RHINOCEROS · THE CHAIRS
THE LESSON

Eugène Ionesco was born in Slatina, Rumania, in 1912, of a Rumanian father and a French mother. He spent much of his childhood in Paris. He returned to Rumania in 1925 where he completed his schooling and studied at the University of Bucharest. He married in 1936 and returned to France two years later. He published poetry and criticism, but did not start writing plays until 1948 when he began to learn English. The phrases contained in an English manual inspired in him a vision of an 'absurd' world, although his first play, *La Cantatrice chauve*, was coldly received. He defined his understanding of the term 'absurd' as 'that which is devoid of purpose ... Cut off from his religious, metaphysical and transcendental roots, man is lost; all his actions become senseless, absurd, useless.' *La Cantatrice chauve*, performed in 1950, was followed by a series of one act plays (including *Le Leçon* and *Les Chaises*) and in 1953 by his first full-length play, *Amédée, ou comment s'en debarasser*. His other plays include *Tueur sans gages* (1957), *Rhinocéros* (1959), *Le Piéton de l'air* (1962), *Le Roi se meurt* (1962), which all feature the character Berenger, *La Soif et la faim* (1965), *Jeux de assacre* (1970), *Macbett* (1972), *Ce Formidable Bordel* (1973), *Homme aux valises* (1975), *Noir et blanc* (1980) and *Journeys Among the Dead* (1986). Martin Esslin once described Ionesco as 'a serious artist dedicated to the arduous exploration of the realities of the human situation, fully aware of the task that he has undertaken, and equipped with formidable intellectual powers.' Ionesco won several major international awards and is acknowledged as one of the most important figures in the history of *avant-garde* theatre. He died in March 1994.

Translated by Donald Keene

Eugène Ionesco

RHINOCEROS
Translated by Derek Prouse

THE CHAIRS · THE LESSON
Translated by Donald Watson

PENGUIN BOOKS

PENGUIN BOOKS

Published by the Penguin Group
Penguin Books Ltd, 27 Wrights Lane, London W8 5TZ, England
Penguin Books USA Inc., 375 Hudson Street, New York, New York 10014, USA
Penguin Books Australia Ltd, Ringwood, Victoria, Australia
Penguin Books Canada Ltd, 10 Alcorn Avenue, Toronto, Ontario, Canada M4V 3B2
Penguin Books (NZ) Ltd, 182–190 Wairau Road, Auckland 10, New Zealand

Penguin Books Ltd, Registered Offices: Harmondsworth, Middlesex, England

Rhinoceros: First published 1959
This translation first published by John Calder 1960
Copyright © John Calder (Publishers) Ltd, 1960

Les Chaises: First published 1954
This translation first published by John Calder 1958
Copyright © John Calder (Publishers) Ltd, 1958

La Leçon: First published 1954
This translation first published by John Calder 1958
Copyright © John Calder (Publishers) Ltd, 1958

Published in Penguin Books 1962
21 23 25 27 29 30 28 26 24 22

Set in Monotype Bembo
Printed in England by Clays Ltd, St Ives plc

Amateur performing rights in these plays are controlled by Samuel French Ltd,
52 Fitzroy Street, London W1P 6JR, and no performance may be given
unless a licence has been obtained. Fees will be quoted on request.
Professional performing rights are controlled by SACD, 9, rue Ballu 75442.
Paris, to whom applications for a licence should be made.

CONTENTS

RHINOCEROS

A Play in Three Acts
and Four Scenes

RHINOCEROS

First produced in Paris by Jean-Louis Barrault at the Odéon, 25 January 1960.

First produced in London by Orson Welles at the Royal Court Theatre, 28 April 1960.

Characters of the Play

JEAN
BERENGER
THE WAITRESS
THE GROCER
THE GROCER'S WIFE
THE OLD GENTLEMAN
THE LOGICIAN
THE HOUSEWIFE
THE CAFÉ PROPRIETOR
DAISY
MR PAPILLON
DUDARD
BOTARD
MRS BOEUF
A FIREMAN
THE LITTLE OLD MAN
THE LITTLE OLD MAN'S WIFE
And a lot of Rhinoceros heads

ACT ONE

The scene is a square in a small provincial town. Up-stage a house composed of a ground floor and one storey. The ground floor is the window of a grocer's shop. The entrance is up two or three steps through a glass-paned door. The word ÉPICERIE *is written in bold letters above the shop window. The two windows on the first floor are the living quarters of the grocer and his wife. The shop is up-stage, but slightly to the left, not far from the wings. In the distance a church steeple is visible above the grocer's house. Between the shop and the left of the stage there is a little street in perspective. To the right, slightly at an angle, is the front of a café. Above the café, one floor with a window; in front, the café terrace; several chairs and tables reach almost to centre stage. A dusty tree stands near the terrace chairs. Blue sky; harsh light; very white walls. The time is almost midday on a Sunday in summertime. Jean and Berenger will sit at one of the terrace tables.*

> [*The sound of church bells is heard, which stop a few moments before the curtain rises. When the curtain rises, a woman carrying a basket of provisions under one arm and a cat under the other crosses the stage in silence from right to left. As she does so, the* GROCER'S WIFE *opens her shop door and watches her pass.*]

GROCER'S WIFE: Oh that woman gets on my nerves! [*To her husband who is in the shop*] Too stuck-up to buy from us nowadays. [*The* GROCER'S WIFE *leaves; the stage is empty for a few moments.*]

> [JEAN *enters right, at the same time as* BERENGER *enters left.* JEAN *is very fastidiously dressed: brown suit, red tie, stiff collar, brown hat. He has a reddish face. His shoes are yellow*

9

and well-polished. BERENGER *is unshaven and hatless, with unkempt hair and creased clothes; everything about him indicates negligence. He seems weary, half-asleep; from time to time he yawns.*]

JEAN [*advancing from right*]: Oh, so you managed to get here at last, Berenger!

BERENGER [*advancing from left*]: Morning, Jean!

JEAN: Late as usual, of course. [*He looks at his wrist-watch.*] Our appointment was for 11.30. And now it's practically mid-day.

BERENGER: I'm sorry. Have you been waiting long?

JEAN: No, I've only just arrived myself, as you saw.

[*They go and sit at one of the tables on the café terrace.*]

BERENGER: In that case I don't feel so bad, if you've only just ...

JEAN: It's different with me. I don't like waiting: I've no time to waste. And as you're never on time, I come late on purpose – at a time when I presume you'll be there.

BERENGER: You're right ... quite right, but ...

JEAN: Now don't try to pretend you're ever on time!

BERENGER: No, of course not ... I wouldn't say that.

[JEAN *and* BERENGER *have sat down.*]

JEAN: There you are, you see!

BERENGER: What are you drinking?

JEAN: You mean to say you've got a thirst even at this time in the morning?

BERENGER: It's so hot and dry.

JEAN: The more you drink the thirstier you get, popular science tells us that ...

BERENGER: It would be less dry, and we'd be less thirsty, if they'd invent us some scientific clouds in the sky.

JEAN [*studying Berenger closely*]: That wouldn't help you any. You're not thirsty for water, Berenger ...

BERENGER: I don't understand what you mean.

JEAN: You know perfectly well what I mean. I'm talking about your parched throat. That's a territory that can't get enough!

BERENGER: To compare my throat to a piece of land seems ...

JEAN [*interrupting him*]: You're in a bad way, my friend.

BERENGER: In a bad way? You think so?

JEAN: I'm not blind, you know. You're dropping with fatigue. You've gone without your sleep again, you yawn all the time, you're dead-tired ...

BERENGER: There is something the matter with my hair ...

JEAN: You reek of alcohol.

BERENGER: I have got a bit of a hang-over, it's true!

JEAN: It's the same every Sunday morning – not to mention the other days of the week.

BERENGER: Oh no, it's less frequent during the week, because of the office ...

JEAN: And what's happened to your tie? Lost it during your orgy, I suppose!

BERENGER [*putting his hand to his neck*]: You're right. That's funny! Whatever could I have done with it?

JEAN [*taking a tie out of his coat pocket*]: Here, put this one on.

BERENGER: Oh thank you, that is kind. [*He puts on the tie.*]

JEAN [*while* BERENGER *is unskilfully tying his tie*]: Your hair's all over the place.

[BERENGER *runs his fingers through his hair.*]

Here, here's a comb! [*He takes a comb from his other pocket.*]

BERENGER [*taking the comb*]: Thank you. [*He vaguely combs his hair.*]

JEAN: You haven't even shaved! Just take a look at yourself!

[*He takes a mirror from his inside pocket, hands it to* BEREN-GER, *who takes a look at himself; as he does so, he examines his tongue.*]

BERENGER: My tongue's all coated.

JEAN [*taking the mirror and putting it back in his pocket*]: I'm not surprised! [*He takes back the comb as well, which* BERENGER *offers to him, and puts it in his pocket.*] You're heading for cirrhosis, my friend.

BERENGER [*worried*]: Do you think so?

JEAN [*to Berenger, who wants to give him back his tie*]: Keep the tie, I've got plenty more.

BERENGER [*admiringly*]: You always look so immaculate.

JEAN [*continuing his inspection of Berenger*]: Your clothes are all crumpled, they're a disgrace! Your shirt is downright filthy, and your shoes ... [BERENGER *tries to hide his feet under the table.*] Your shoes haven't been touched. What a mess you're in! And look at your shoulders ...

BERENGER: What's the matter with my shoulders?

JEAN: Turn round! Come on, turn round! You've been leaning against some wall. [BERENGER *holds his hand out docilely to Jean.*] No, I haven't got a brush with me; it would make my pockets bulge. [*Still docile,* BERENGER *flicks his shoulders to get rid of the white dust;* JEAN *averts his head.*] Heavens! Where did you get all that from?

BERENGER: I don't remember.

JEAN: It's a positive disgrace! I feel ashamed to be your friend.

BERENGER: You're very hard on me ...

JEAN: I've every reason to be.

BERENGER: Listen, Jean. There are so few distractions in this town – I get so bored. I'm not made for the work I'm doing ... every day at the office, eight hours a day – and only three weeks' holiday a year! When Saturday night comes round I feel exhausted and so – you know how it is – just to relax ...

JEAN: My dear man, everybody has to work. I spend eight hours a day in the office the same as everyone else. And I only get three weeks off a year, but even so you don't catch me ... Will-power, my good man!

BERENGER: But everybody hasn't got as much will-power as you have. I can't get used to it. I just can't get used to life.

JEAN: Everybody has to get used to it. Or do you consider yourself some superior being?

BERENGER: I don't pretend to be …

JEAN [*interrupting him*]: I'm just as good as you are; I think with all due modesty I may say I'm better. The superior man is the man who fulfils his duty.

BERENGER: What duty?

JEAN: His duty … His duty as an employee, for example.

BERENGER: Oh yes, his duty as an employee …

JEAN: Where did your debauch take place last night? If you can remember!

BERENGER: We were celebrating Auguste's birthday, our friend Auguste …

JEAN: Our friend Auguste? Nobody invited me to our friend Auguste's birthday …

[*At this moment a noise is heard, far off, but swiftly approaching, of a beast panting in its headlong course, and of a long trumpeting.*]

BERENGER: I couldn't refuse. It wouldn't have been nice …

JEAN: Did I go there?

BERENGER: Well, perhaps it was because you weren't invited.

WAITRESS [*coming out of café*]: Good morning, gentlemen. Can I get you something to drink?

[*The noise becomes very loud.*]

JEAN [*to Berenger, almost shouting to make himself heard above the noise which he has not become conscious of*]: True, I was not invited. That honour was denied me. But in any case, I can assure you, that even if I had been invited, I would not have gone, because …

[*The noise has become intense.*]

What's going on?

[*The noise of a powerful, heavy animal, galloping at great speed, is heard very close; the sound of panting.*]

Whatever is it?

WAITRESS: Whatever is it?

[BERENGER, *still listless without appearing to hear anything at all, replies tranquilly to Jean about the invitation; his lips move but one doesn't hear what he says;* JEAN *bounds to his feet, knocking his chair over as he does so, looks off left pointing, whilst* BERENGER, *still a little dopey, remains seated.*]

JEAN: Oh, a rhinoceros!

[*The noise made by the animal dies away swiftly and one can already hear the following words. The whole of this scene must be played very fast, each repeating in swift succession:* 'Oh, a rhinoceros!']

WAITRESS: Oh, a rhinoceros!

GROCER'S WIFE [*sticks her head out of her shop doorway*]: Oh, a rhinoceros! [*To her husband still inside the shop*] Quick, come and look; it's a rhinoceros!

[*They are all looking off left after the animal.*]

JEAN: It's rushing straight ahead, brushing up against the shop windows.

GROCER [*in his shop*]: Whereabouts?

WAITRESS [*putting her hands on her hips*]: Well!

GROCER'S WIFE [*to her husband who is still in shop*]: Come and look!

[*At this moment the* GROCER *puts his head out.*]

GROCER: Oh, a rhinoceros!

LOGICIAN [*entering quickly left*]: A rhinoceros going full-tilt on the opposite pavement!

[*All these speeches from the time when* JEAN *says* 'Oh, a rhinoceros' *are practically simultaneous. A woman is heard crying* 'Ah!' *She appears. She runs to the centre-stage; it is a* HOUSEWIFE *with a basket on her arm; once arrived centre-stage she drops her basket; the contents scatter all over the stage, a bottle breaks, but she does not drop her cat.*]

HOUSEWIFE: Ah! Oh!

[*An elegant* OLD GENTLEMAN *comes from left stage, after the*

Housewife, rushes into the Grocer's shop, knocks into the Grocer and his Wife, whilst the LOGICIAN *installs himself against the back wall on the left of the grocery entrance.* JEAN *and the* WAITRESS, *standing, and* BERENGER, *still apathetically seated, together form another group. At the same time, coming from the left, cries of 'Oh' and 'Ah' and the noise of people running have been heard. The dust raised by the animal spreads over the stage.*]

CAFÉ PROPRIETOR [*sticking his head out of the first-floor window*]: What's going on?

OLD GENTLEMAN [*disappearing behind the Grocer and his Wife*]: Excuse me, please!

[*The* OLD GENTLEMAN *is elegantly dressed, with white spats, a soft hat, and an ivory-handled cane; the* LOGICIAN, *propped up against the wall, has a little grey moustache, an eyeglass, and is wearing a straw hat.*]

GROCER'S WIFE [*jostled and jostling her husband; to the Old Gentleman*]: Watch out with that stick!

GROCER: Look where you're going, can't you!

[*The head of the Old Gentleman is seen behind the Grocer and his Wife.*]

WAITRESS [*to the Proprietor*]: A rhinoceros!

PROPRIETOR [*to the Waitress from his window*]: You're seeing things. [*He sees the rhinoceros*] Well, I'll be ...!

HOUSEWIFE: Ah!

[*The 'Ohs' and 'Ahs' from off-stage form a background accompaniment to her 'Ah'. She has dropped her basket, her provisions, and the bottle, but has nevertheless kept tight hold of her cat which she carries under her other arm.*]

There, they frightened the poor pussy!

PROPRIETOR [*still looking off left, following the distant course of the animal as the noises fade; hooves, trumpetings, etc.* BERENGER *sleepily averts his head a little on account of the dust, but says nothing; he simply makes a grimace*]: Well, of all things!

JEAN [*also averting his head a little, but very much awake*]: Well, of all things! [*He sneezes.*]

HOUSEWIFE [*she is centre-stage but turned towards left; her provisions scattered on the ground round her*]: Well of all things! [*She sneezes.*]

[*The* OLD GENTLEMAN, GROCER'S WIFE, *and* GROCER *up-stage re-opening the glass door of the Grocer's shop that the Old Gentleman has closed behind him.*]

ALL THREE: Well, of all things!

JEAN: Well, of all things! [*To Berenger*] Did you see that?

[*The noise of the rhinoceros and its trumpeting are now far away; the people are still staring after the animal, all except for* BERENGER *who is still apathetically seated.*]

ALL [*except Berenger*]: Well, of all things!

BERENGER [*to Jean*]: It certainly looked as if it was a rhinoceros. It made plenty of dust. [*He takes out a handkerchief and blows his nose.*]

HOUSEWIFE: Well, of all things! Gave me such a scare.

GROCER [*to the Housewife*]: Your basket ... and all your things ...

[*The* OLD GENTLEMAN *approaches the lady and bends to pick up her things scattered about the stage. He greets her gallantly, raising his hat.*]

PROPRIETOR: Really, these days, you never know ...

WAITRESS: Fancy that!

OLD GENTLEMAN [*to the Housewife*]: May I help you pick up your things?

HOUSEWIFE [*to the Old Gentleman*]: Thank you, how very kind! Do put on your hat. Oh, it gave me such a scare!

LOGICIAN: Fear is an irrational thing. It must yield to reason.

WAITRESS: It's already out of sight.

OLD GENTLEMAN [*to the Housewife and indicating the Logician*]: My friend is a logician.

JEAN [*to Berenger*]: Well, what did you think of that?

WAITRESS: Those animals can certainly travel!

HOUSEWIFE [to the Logician]: Very happy to meet you!

GROCER'S WIFE [to the Grocer]: That'll teach her to buy her things from somebody else!

JEAN [to the Proprietor and the Waitress]: What did you think of that?

HOUSEWIFE: I still didn't let my cat go.

PROPRIETOR [shrugging his shoulders, at window]: You don't often see that!

HOUSEWIFE [to the Logician and the Old Gentleman who is picking up her provisions]: Would you hold him a moment!

WAITRESS [to Jean]: First time I've seen that!

LOGICIAN [to the Housewife, taking the cat in his arms]: It's not spiteful is it?

PROPRIETOR [to Jean]: Went past like a comet!

HOUSEWIFE [to the Logician]: He wouldn't hurt a fly. [To the others.] What happened to my wine?

GROCER [to the Housewife]: I've got plenty more.

JEAN [to Berenger]: Well, what did you think of that?

GROCER [to the Housewife]: And good stuff, too!

PROPRIETOR [to the Waitress]: Don't hang about! Look after these gentlemen! [He indicates Berenger and Jean. He withdraws.]

BERENGER [to Jean]: What did I think of what?

GROCER'S WIFE [to the Grocer]: Go and get her another bottle!

JEAN [to Berenger]: Of the rhinoceros, of course! What did you think I meant?

GROCER [to the Housewife]: I've got some first-class wine, in unbreakable bottles! [He disappears into his shop.]

LOGICIAN [stroking the cat in his arms]: Puss, puss, puss.

WAITRESS [to Berenger and Jean]: What are you drinking?

BERENGER: Two pastis.

WAITRESS: Two pastis – right! [She walks to the café entrance.]

HOUSEWIFE [*picking up her things with the help of the Old Gentleman*]: Very kind of you, I'm sure.

WAITRESS: Two pastis! [*She goes into café.*]

OLD GENTLEMAN [*to the Housewife*]: Oh, please don't mention it, it's a pleasure.

[*The* GROCER'S WIFE *goes into shop.*]

LOGICIAN [*to the Old Gentleman and the Housewife picking up the provisions*]: Replace them in an orderly fashion.

JEAN [*to Berenger*]: Well, what did you think about it?

BERENGER [*to Jean, not knowing what to say*]: Well ... nothing ... it made a lot of dust ...

GROCER [*coming out of shop with a bottle of wine; to the Housewife*]: I've some good leeks as well.

LOGICIAN [*still stroking the cat*]: Puss, puss, puss.

GROCER [*to the Housewife*]: It's a hundred francs a litre.

HOUSEWIFE [*paying the Grocer, then to the Old Gentleman who has managed to put everything back in the basket*]: Oh, you are kind! Such a pleasure to come across the old French courtesy. Not like the young people today!

GROCER [*taking money*]: You should buy from me. You wouldn't even have to cross the street, and you wouldn't run the risk of these accidents. [*He goes back into his shop.*]

JEAN [*who has sat down and is still thinking of the rhinoceros*]: But you must admit it's extraordinary.

OLD GENTLEMAN [*taking off his hat, and kissing the Housewife's hand*]: It was a great pleasure to meet you!

HOUSEWIFE [*to the Logician*]: Thank you very much for holding my cat.

[*The* LOGICIAN *gives the Housewife back her cat. The* WAITRESS *comes back with drinks.*]

WAITRESS: Two pastis!

JEAN [*to Berenger*]: You're incorrigible!

OLD GENTLEMAN [*to the Housewife*]: May I accompany you part of the way?

BERENGER [*to Jean, and pointing to the* WAITRESS *who goes back into the café*]: I asked for mineral water. She's made a mistake.

[JEAN, *scornful and disbelieving, shrugs his shoulders.*]

HOUSEWIFE [*to the Old Gentleman*]: My husband's waiting for me, thank you. Perhaps some other time ...

OLD GENTLEMAN [*to the Housewife*]: I sincerely hope so, Madame.

HOUSEWIFE [*to the Old Gentleman*]: So do I! [*She gives him a sweet look as she leaves left.*]

BERENGER: The dust's settled ...

[JEAN *shrugs his shoulders again.*]

OLD GENTLEMAN [*to the Logician, and looking after the Housewife*]: Delightful creature!

JEAN [*to Berenger*]: A rhinoceros! I can't get over it!

[*The* OLD GENTLEMAN *and the* LOGICIAN *move slowly right and off. They chat amiably.*]

OLD GENTLEMAN [*to the Logician, after casting a fond look after the Housewife*]: Charming, isn't she?

LOGICIAN [*to the Old Gentleman*]: I'm going to explain to you what a syllogism is.

OLD GENTLEMAN: Ah yes, a syllogism.

JEAN [*to Berenger*]: I can't get over it! It's unthinkable!

[BERENGER *yawns.*]

LOGICIAN: A syllogism consists of a main proposition, a secondary one, and a conclusion.

OLD GENTLEMAN: What conclusion?

[*The* LOGICIAN *and the* OLD GENTLEMAN *go out.*]

JEAN: I just can't get over it.

BERENGER: Yes, I can see you can't. Well, it was a rhinoceros – all right, so it was a rhinoceros! It's miles away by now ... miles away ...

JEAN: But you must see it's fantastic! A rhinoceros loose in the town, and you don't bat an eyelid! It shouldn't be allowed!

[BERENGER *yawns.*]

Put your hand in front of your mouth!

BERENGER: Yais ... yais ... It shouldn't be allowed. It's dangerous. I hadn't realized. But don't worry about it, it won't get us here.

JEAN: We ought to protest to the Town Council! What's the Council there for?

BERENGER [*yawning, then quickly putting his hand to his mouth*]: Oh excuse me ... perhaps the rhinoceros escaped from the zoo.

JEAN: You're day-dreaming.

BERENGER: But I'm wide awake.

JEAN: Awake or asleep, it's the same thing.

BERENGER: But there is some difference.

JEAN: That's not the point.

BERENGER: But you just said being awake and being asleep were the same thing ...

JEAN: You didn't understand. There's no difference between dreaming awake and dreaming asleep.

BERENGER: I do dream. Life is a dream.

JEAN: You're certainly dreaming when you say the rhinoceros escaped from the zoo ...

BERENGER: I only said: perhaps.

JEAN: ... because there's been no zoo in our town since the animals were destroyed in the plague ... ages ago ...

BERENGER [*with the same indifference*]: Then perhaps it came from a circus.

JEAN: What circus are you talking about?

BERENGER: I don't know ... some travelling circus.

JEAN: You know perfectly well that the Council banned all travelling performers from the district ... There haven't been any since we were children.

BERENGER [*trying unsuccessfully to stop yawning*]: In that case, maybe it's been hiding ever since in the surrounding swamps?

JEAN: The surrounding swamps! The surrounding swamps! My poor friend, you live in a thick haze of alcohol.

BERENGER [*naïvely*]: That's very true ... it seems to mount from my stomach ...

JEAN: It's clouding your brain! Where do you know of any surrounding swamps? Our district is known as 'little Castille' because the land is so arid.

BERENGER [*surfeited and pretty weary*]: How do I know, then? Perhaps it's been hiding under a stone? ... Or maybe it's been nesting on some withered branch?

JEAN: If you think you're being witty, you're very much mistaken! You're just being a bore with ... with your stupid paradoxes. You're incapable of talking seriously!

BERENGER: Today, yes, only today ... because of ... because of ... [*He indicates his head with a vague gesture.*]

JEAN: Today the same as any other day!

BERENGER: Oh, not quite as much.

JEAN: Your witticisms are not very inspired.

BERENGER: I wasn't trying to be ...

JEAN [*interrupting him*]: I can't bear people to try and make fun of me!

BERENGER [*hand on his heart*]: But my dear Jean, I'd never allow myself to ...

JEAN [*interrupting him*]: My dear Berenger, you are allowing yourself ...

BERENGER: Oh no, never. I'd never allow myself to.

JEAN: Yes, you would; you've just done so.

BERENGER: But how could you possibly think ...

JEAN [*interrupting him*]: I think what is true!

BERENGER: But I assure you ...

JEAN [*interrupting him*]: ... that you were making fun of me!

BERENGER: You really can be obstinate, sometimes.

JEAN: And now you're calling me a mule into the bargain. Even you must see how insulting you're being.

BERENGER: It would never have entered my mind.

JEAN: You have no mind!

BERENGER: All the more reason why it would never enter it.

JEAN: There are certain things which enter the minds even of people without one.

BERENGER: That's impossible.

JEAN: And why, pray, is it impossible?

BERENGER: Because it's impossible.

JEAN: Then kindly explain to me why it's impossible, as you seem to imagine you can explain everything.

BERENGER: I don't imagine anything of the kind.

JEAN: Then why do you act as if you do? And, I repeat, why are you being so insulting to me?

BERENGER: I'm not insulting you. Far from it. You know what tremendous respect I have for you.

JEAN: In that case, why do you contradict me, making out that it's not dangerous to let a rhinoceros go racing about in the middle of the town – particularly on a Sunday morning when the streets are full of children ... and adults, too ...

BERENGER: A lot of them are in church. They don't run any risk ...

JEAN [interrupting him]: If you will allow me to finish ... and at market time, too.

BERENGER: I never said it wasn't dangerous to let a rhinoceros go racing about the town. I simply said I'd personally never considered the danger. It had never crossed my mind.

JEAN: You never consider anything.

BERENGER: All right, I agree. A rhinoceros roaming about is not a good thing.

JEAN: It shouldn't be allowed.

BERENGER: I agree. It shouldn't be allowed. It's a ridiculous thing all right! But it's no reason for you and me to quarrel. Why go on at me just because some wretched perissodactyle happens to pass by. A stupid quadruped not worth talking about. And ferocious into the bargain. And which has already disappeared, which doesn't exist any longer. We're not going to bother about some animal that doesn't exist. Let's talk about something else, Jean, please; [*He yawns.*] there are plenty of other subjects for conversation. [*He takes his glass.*] To you!

[*At this moment the* LOGICIAN *and the* OLD GENTLEMAN *come back on stage from left; they walk over, talking as they go, to one of the tables on the café terrace, some distance from Berenger and Jean, behind and to the right of them.*]

JEAN: Put that glass back on the table! You're not to drink it.

[JEAN *takes a large swallow from his own pastis and puts back the glass, half-empty, on the table.* BERENGER *continues to hold his glass, without putting it down, and without daring to drink from it either.*]

BERENGER [*timidly*]: There's no point in leaving it for the proprietor. [*He makes as if to drink.*]

JEAN: Put it down, I tell you!

BERENGER: Very well.

[*He is putting the glass back on the table when* DAISY *passes. She is a young blonde typist and she crosses the stage from right to left. When he sees her,* BERENGER *rises abruptly, and in doing so makes an awkward movement; the glass falls and splashes Jean's trousers.*]

Oh, there's Daisy!

JEAN: Look out! How clumsy you are!

BERENGER: That's Daisy ... I'm so sorry ... [*He hides himself out of sight of Daisy.*] I don't want her to see me in this state.

JEAN: Your behaviour's unforgivable, absolutely unforgivable! [*He looks in the direction of* DAISY, *who is just disappearing.*] Why are you afraid of that young girl?

BERENGER: Oh, be quiet, please be quiet!

JEAN: She doesn't look an unpleasant person!

BERENGER [*coming back to Jean, now that Daisy has gone*]: I must apologize once more for …

JEAN: You see what comes of drinking, you can no longer control your movements, you've no strength left in your hands, you're besotted and fagged out. You're digging your own grave, my friend, you're destroying yourself.

BERENGER: I don't like the taste of alcohol much. And yet if I don't drink, I'm done for; it's as if I'm frightened, and so I drink not to be frightened any longer.

JEAN: Frightened of what?

BERENGER: I don't know exactly. It's a sort of anguish difficult to describe. I feel out of place in life, among people, and so I take to drink. That calms me down and relaxes me so I can forget.

JEAN: You try to escape from yourself!

BERENGER: I'm so tired, I've been tired for years. It's exhausting to drag the weight of my own body about …

JEAN: That's alcoholic neurasthenia, drinker's gloom …

BERENGER [*continuing*]: I'm conscious of my body all the time, as if it were made of lead, or as if I were carrying another man around on my back. I can't seem to get used to myself. I don't even know if I *am* me. Then as soon as I take a drink, the lead slips away and I recognize myself, I become me again.

JEAN: That's just being fanciful. Look at me, Berenger, I weigh more than you do. And yet I feel light, light as a feather! [*He flaps his arms as if about to fly. The* OLD GENTLE-MAN *and the* LOGICIAN *have come back and have taken a few steps on the stage deep in talk. At this moment they are passing by Jean and Berenger.* JEAN'S *arm deals the* OLD GENTLEMAN *a sharp knock which precipitates him into the arms of the Logician.*]

LOGICIAN: An example of a syllogism … [*He is knocked.*] Oh!

OLD GENTLEMAN [*to Jean*]: Look out! [*To the Logician*] I'm so sorry.

JEAN [*to the Old Gentleman*]: I'm so sorry.

LOGICIAN [*to the Old Gentleman*]: No harm done.

OLD GENTLEMAN [*to Jean*]: No harm done.

[*The* OLD GENTLEMAN *and the* LOGICIAN *go and sit at one of the terrace tables a little to the right and behind Jean and Berenger.*]

BERENGER [*to Jean*]: You certainly are strong.

JEAN: Yes, I'm strong. I'm strong for several reasons. In the first place I'm strong because I'm naturally strong, and secondly I'm strong because I have moral strength. I'm also strong because I'm not riddled with alcohol. I don't wish to offend you, my dear Berenger, but I feel I must tell you that it's alcohol which weighs so heavy on you.

LOGICIAN [*to the Old Gentleman*]: Here is an example of a syllogism. The cat has four paws. Isidore and Fricot both have four paws. Therefore Isidore and Fricot are cats.

OLD GENTLEMAN [*to the Logician*]: My dog has got four paws.

LOGICIAN [*to the Old Gentleman*]: Then it's a cat.

BERENGER [*to Jean*]: I've barely got the strength to go on living. Maybe I don't even want to.

OLD GENTLEMAN [*to the Logician, after deep reflection*]: So then logically speaking, my dog must be a cat?

LOGICIAN [*to the Old Gentleman*]: Logically, yes. But the contrary is also true.

BERENGER [*to Jean*]: Solitude seems to oppress me. And so does the company of other people.

JEAN [*to Berenger*]: You contradict yourself. What oppresses you – solitude, or the company of others? You consider yourself a thinker, yet you're devoid of logic.

OLD GENTLEMAN [*to the Logician*]: Logic is a very beautiful thing.

LOGICIAN [*to the Old Gentleman*]: As long as it is not abused.

BERENGER [*to Jean*]: Life is an abnormal business.

JEAN: On the contrary. Nothing could be more natural, and the proof is that people go on living.

BERENGER: There are more dead people than living. And their numbers are increasing. The living are getting rarer.

JEAN: The dead don't exist, there's no getting away from that! ... Ah! Ah ...! [*He gives a huge laugh.*] Yet you're oppressed by them, too? How can you be oppressed by something that doesn't exist?

BERENGER: I sometimes wonder if I exist myself.

JEAN: You don't exist, my dear Berenger, because you don't think. Start thinking, then you will.

LOGICIAN [*to the Old Gentleman*]: Another syllogism. All cats die. Socrates is dead. Therefore Socrates is a cat.

OLD GENTLEMAN: And he's got four paws. That's true. I've got a cat named Socrates.

LOGICIAN: There you are, you see ...

JEAN [*to Berenger*]: Fundamentally you're just a bluffer. And a liar. You say that life doesn't interest you. And yet there's somebody who does.

BERENGER: Who?

JEAN: Your little friend from the office who just went past. You're very fond of her!

OLD GENTLEMAN [*to the Logician*]: So Socrates was a cat, was he?

LOGICIAN: Logic has just revealed the fact to us.

JEAN [*to Berenger*]: You didn't want her to see you in your present state. [BERENGER *makes a gesture.*] That proves you're not indifferent to everything. But how can you expect Daisy to be attracted to a drunkard?

LOGICIAN [*to the Old Gentleman*]: Let's get back to our cats.

OLD GENTLEMAN [*to the Logician*]: I'm all ears.

BERENGER [*to Jean*]: In any case, I think she's already got her eye on someone.

JEAN: Oh, who?

BERENGER: Dudard. An office colleague, qualified in law, with a big future in the firm – and in Daisy's affections. I can't hope to compete with him.

LOGICIAN [*to the Old Gentleman*]: The cat Isidore has four paws.

OLD GENTLEMAN: How do you know?

LOGICIAN: It's stated in the hypothesis.

BERENGER [*to Jean*]: The Chief thinks a lot of him. Whereas I've no future, I've no qualifications. I don't stand a chance.

OLD GENTLEMAN [*to the Logician*]: Ah! In the hypothesis.

JEAN [*to Berenger*]: So you're giving up, just like that ...?

BERENGER: What else can I do?

LOGICIAN [*to the Old Gentleman*]: Fricot also has four paws. So how many paws have Fricot and Isidore?

OLD GENTLEMAN: Separately or together?

JEAN [*to Berenger*]: Life is a struggle, it's cowardly not to put up a fight!

LOGICIAN [*to the Old Gentleman*]: Separately or together, it all depends.

BERENGER [*to Jean*]: What can I do? I've nothing to put up a fight with.

JEAN: Then find yourself some weapons, my friend.

OLD GENTLEMAN [*to the Logician, after painful reflection*]: Eight, eight paws.

LOGICIAN: Logic involves mental arithmetic, you see.

OLD GENTLEMAN: It certainly has many aspects!

BERENGER [*to Jean*]: Where can I find the weapons?

LOGICIAN [*to the Old Gentleman*]: There are no limits to logic.

JEAN: Within yourself. Through your own will.

BERENGER: What weapons?

LOGICIAN [*to the Old Gentleman*]: I'm going to show you ...

JEAN [*to Berenger*]: The weapons of patience and culture, the weapons of the mind. [BERENGER *yawns*.] Turn yourself

into a keen and brilliant intellect. Get yourself up to the
mark!

BERENGER: How do I get myself up to the mark?

LOGICIAN [to the Old Gentleman]: If I take two paws away
from these cats – how many does each have left?

OLD GENTLEMAN: That's not so easy.

BERENGER [to Jean]: That's not so easy.

LOGICIAN [to the Old Gentleman]: On the contrary, it's simple.

OLD GENTLEMAN [to the Logician]: It may be simple for you,
but not for me.

BERENGER [to Jean]: It may be simple for you, but not for
me.

LOGICIAN [to the Old Gentleman]: Come on, exercise your
mind. Concentrate!

JEAN [to Berenger]: Come on, exercise your will. Concentrate!

OLD GENTLEMAN [to the Logician]: I don't see how.

BERENGER [to Jean]: I really don't see how.

LOGICIAN [to the Old Gentleman]: You have to be told everything.

JEAN [to Berenger]: You have to be told everything.

LOGICIAN [to the Old Gentleman]: Take a sheet of paper and
calculate. If you take six paws from the two cats, how many
paws are left to each cat?

OLD GENTLEMAN: Just a moment ... [He calculates on a sheet of
paper which he takes from his pocket.]

JEAN: This is what you must do: dress yourself properly,
shave every day, put on a clean shirt.

BERENGER: The laundry's so expensive ...

JEAN: Cut down on your drinking. This is the way to come
out: wear a hat, a tie like this, a well-cut suit, shoes well
polished. [As he mentions the various items of clothing he points
self-contentedly to his own hat, tie, and shoes.]

OLD GENTLEMAN [to the Logician]: There are several possible
solutions.

LOGICIAN [*to the Old Gentleman*]: Tell me.

BERENGER [*to Jean*]: Then what do I do? Tell me ...

LOGICIAN [*to the Old Gentleman*]: I'm listening.

BERENGER [*to Jean*]: I'm listening.

JEAN: You're a timid creature, but not without talent.

BERENGER: I've got talent, me?

JEAN: So use it. Put yourself in the picture. Keep abreast of the cultural and literary events of the times.

OLD GENTLEMAN [*to the Logician*]: One possibility is: one cat could have four paws and the other two.

BERENGER [*to Jean*]: I get so little spare time!

LOGICIAN [*to the Old Gentleman*]: You're not without talent. You just needed to exercise it.

JEAN: Take advantage of what free time you *do* have. Don't just let yourself drift.

OLD GENTLEMAN: I've never had the time. I was an official, you know.

LOGICIAN: One can always find time to learn.

JEAN [*to Berenger*]: One can always find time.

BERENGER [*to Jean*]: It's too late now.

OLD GENTLEMAN [*to the Logician*]: It's a bit late in the day for me.

JEAN [*to Berenger*]: It's never too late.

LOGICIAN [*to the Old Gentleman*]: It's never too late.

JEAN [*to Berenger*]: You work eight hours a day, like me and everybody else, but not on Sundays, nor in the evening, nor for three weeks in the summer. That's quite sufficient, with a little method.

LOGICIAN [*to the Old Gentleman*]: Well, what about the other solutions? Use a little method, a little method!

[*The* OLD GENTLEMAN *starts to calculate anew.*]

JEAN [*to Berenger*]: Look, instead of drinking and feeling sick, isn't it better to be fresh and eager, even at work? And you can spend your free time constructively.

BERENGER: How do you mean?

JEAN: By visiting museums, reading literary periodicals, going to lectures. That'll solve your troubles, it will develop your mind. In four weeks you'll be a cultured man.

BERENGER: You're right.

OLD GENTLEMAN [to the Logician]: There could be one cat with five paws ...

JEAN [to Berenger]: You see, you even think so yourself!

OLD GENTLEMAN [to the Logician]: And one cat with one paw. But would they still be cats, then?

LOGICIAN [to the Old Gentleman]: Why not?

JEAN [to Berenger]: Instead of squandering all your spare money on drink, isn't it better to buy a ticket for an interesting play? Do you know anything about the avant-garde theatre there's so much talk about? Have you seen Ionesco's plays?

BERENGER [to Jean]: Unfortunately, no. I've only heard people talk about them.

OLD GENTLEMAN [to the Logician]: By taking two of the eight paws away from the two cats ...

JEAN [to Berenger]: There's one playing now. Take advantage of it.

OLD GENTLEMAN [to the Logician]: ... we could have one cat with six paws ...

BERENGER: It would be an excellent initiation into the artistic life of our times.

OLD GENTLEMAN [to the Logician]: We could have one cat with no paws at all.

BERENGER: You're right, perfectly right. I'm going to put myself into the picture, like you said.

LOGICIAN [to the Old Gentleman]: In that case, one cat would be specially privileged.

BERENGER [to Jean]: I will, I promise you.

JEAN: You promise yourself, that's the main thing.

OLD GENTLEMAN: And one under-privileged cat deprived of all paws.

BERENGER: I make myself a solemn promise, I'll keep my word to myself.

LOGICIAN: That would be unjust, and therefore not logical.

BERENGER: Instead of drinking, I'll develop my mind. I feel better already. My head already feels clearer.

JEAN: You see!

OLD GENTLEMAN [to the Logician]: Not logical?

BERENGER: This afternoon I'll go to the museum. And I'll book two seats for the theatre this evening. Will you come with me?

LOGICIAN [to the Old Gentleman]: Because Logic means Justice.

JEAN [to Berenger]: You must persevere. Keep up your good resolutions.

OLD GENTLEMAN [to the Logician]: I get it. Justice ...

BERENGER [to Jean]: I promise you, and I promise myself. Will you come to the museum with me this afternoon?

JEAN [to Berenger]: I have to take a rest this afternoon; it's in my programme for the day.

OLD GENTLEMAN: Justice is one more aspect of Logic.

BERENGER [to Jean]: But you will come with me to the theatre this evening?

JEAN: No, not this evening.

LOGICIAN [to the Old Gentleman]: Your mind is getting clearer!

JEAN [to Berenger]: I sincerely hope you'll keep up your good resolutions. But this evening I have to meet some friends for a drink.

BERENGER: For a drink?

OLD GENTLEMAN [to the Logician]: What's more, a cat with no paws at all ...

JEAN [to Berenger]: I've promised to go. I always keep my word.

OLD GENTLEMAN [*to the Logician*]: ... wouldn't be able to run fast enough to catch mice.

BERENGER [*to Jean*]: Ah, now it's you that's setting me a bad example! You're going out drinking.

LOGICIAN [*to the Old Gentleman*]: You're already making progress in logic.

[*A sound of rapid galloping is heard approaching again, trumpeting and the sound of rhinoceros hooves and pantings; this time the sound comes from the opposite direction approaching from back-stage to front, in the left wings.*]

JEAN [*furiously to Berenger*]: It's not a habit with me, you know. It's not the same as with you. With you ... you're ... it's not the same thing at all ...

BERENGER: Why isn't it the same thing?

JEAN [*shouting over the noise coming from the café*]: I'm no drunkard, not me!

LOGICIAN [*shouting to the Old Gentleman*]: Even with no paws a cat must catch mice. That's in its nature.

BERENGER [*shouting very loudly*]: I didn't mean you were a drunkard. But why would it make me one any more than you, in a case like that?

OLD GENTLEMAN [*shouting to the Logician*]: What's in the cat's nature?

JEAN [*to Berenger*]: Because there's moderation in all things. I'm a moderate person, not like you!

LOGICIAN [*to the Old Gentleman, cupping his hands to his ears*]: What did you say? [*Deafening sounds drown the words of the four characters.*]

BERENGER [*to Jean, cupping his hands to his ears*]: What about me, what? What did you say?

JEAN [*roaring*]: I said that ...

OLD GENTLEMAN [*roaring*]: I said that ...

JEAN [*suddenly aware of the noises which are now very near*]: Whatever's happening?

LOGICIAN: What is going on?

JEAN [*rises, knocking his chair over as he does so; looks towards left wings where the noises of the passing rhinoceros are coming from*]: Oh, a rhinoceros!

LOGICIAN [*rising, knocking over his chair*]: Oh, a rhinoceros!

OLD GENTLEMAN [*doing the same*]: Oh, a rhinoceros!

BERENGER [*still seated, but this time, taking more notice*]: Rhinoceros! In the opposite direction!

WAITRESS [*emerging with a tray and glasses*]: What is it? Oh, a rhinoceros! [*She drops the tray, breaking the glasses.*]

PROPRIETOR [*coming out of the café*]: What's going on?

WAITRESS [*to the Proprietor*]: A rhinoceros!

LOGICIAN: A rhinoceros, going full-tilt on the opposite pavement!

GROCER [*coming out of his shop*]: Oh, a rhinoceros!

JEAN: Oh, a rhinoceros!

GROCER'S WIFE [*sticking her head through the upstairs window of shop*]: Oh, a rhinoceros!

PROPRIETOR: It's no reason to break the glasses.

JEAN: It's rushing straight ahead, brushing up against the shop windows.

DAISY [*entering left*]: Oh, a rhinoceros!

BERENGER [*noticing Daisy*]: Oh, Daisy!
[*noise of people fleeing, the same 'Ohs' and 'Ahs' as before*]

WAITRESS: Well of all things!

PROPRIETOR [*to the Waitress*]: You'll be charged up for those!
[BERENGER *tries to make himself scarce, not to be seen by Daisy. The* OLD GENTLEMAN, *the* LOGICIAN, *the* GROCER, *and his* WIFE *move to centre-stage and say together*]

ALL: Well, of all things!

JEAN *and* BERENGER: Well, of all things!
[*A piteous mewing is heard, then an equally piteous cry of a woman.*]

ALL: Oh!

33

[*Almost at the same time, and as the noises are rapidly dying away the* HOUSEWIFE *appears without her basket but holding the blood-stained corpse of her cat in her arms.*]

HOUSEWIFE [*wailing*]: It ran over my cat, it ran over my cat!

WAITRESS: It ran over her cat!

[*The* GROCER, *his* WIFE [*at the window*], *the* OLD GENTLE-MAN, DAISY, *and the* LOGICIAN *crowd round the* HOUSE-WIFE, *saying*]

ALL: What a tragedy, poor little thing!

OLD GENTLEMAN: Poor little thing!

DAISY *and* WAITRESS: Poor little thing!

GROCER'S WIFE [*at the window*]:
OLD GENTLEMAN: } Poor little thing!
LOGICIAN:

PROPRIETOR [*to the Waitress, pointing to the broken glasses and the upturned chairs*]: Don't just stand there! Clear up the mess!

[JEAN *and* BERENGER *also rush over to the Housewife who continues to lament, her dead cat in her arms.*]

WAITRESS [*moving to the café terrace to pick up the broken glasses and the chairs, and looking over her shoulder at the Housewife*]: Oh, poor little thing!

PROPRIETOR [*pointing, for the Waitress's benefit, to the debris*]: Over there, over there!

OLD GENTLEMAN [*to the Grocer*]: Well, what do you think of that?

BERENGER [*to the Housewife*]: You mustn't cry like that, it's too heartbreaking!

DAISY [*to Berenger*]: Were you there, Mr Berenger? Did you see it?

BERENGER [*to Daisy*]: Good morning, Miss Daisy, you must excuse me, I haven't had a chance to shave ...

PROPRIETOR [*supervising the clearing up of the debris, then glancing towards the Housewife*]: Poor little thing!

WAITRESS [*clearing up the mess, her back to the Housewife*]: Poor little thing!

[*These remarks must obviously be made very rapidly, almost simultaneously.*]

GROCER'S WIFE [*at window*]: That's going too far!

JEAN: That's going too far!

HOUSEWIFE [*lamenting, and cradling the dead cat in her arms*]: My poor little pussy, my poor little cat.

OLD GENTLEMAN [*to the Housewife*]: What can you do, dear lady, cats are only mortal.

LOGICIAN: What do you expect, Madam? All cats are mortal! One must accept that.

HOUSEWIFE [*lamenting*]: My little cat, my poor little cat.

PROPRIETOR [*to the Waitress whose apron is full of broken glass*]: Throw that in the dustbin! [*He has picked up the chairs.*] You owe me a thousand francs.

WAITRESS [*moving into the café*]: All you think of is money!

GROCER'S WIFE [*to the Housewife; from window*]: Don't upset yourself!

OLD GENTLEMAN [*to the Housewife*]: Don't upset yourself, dear lady!

GROCER'S WIFE [*from window*]: It's very upsetting a thing like that!

HOUSEWIFE: My little cat, my little cat!

DAISY: Yes, it's very upsetting a thing like that.

OLD GENTLEMAN [*supporting the Housewife, and guiding her to a table on the terrace followed by the others*]: Sit down here, dear lady.

JEAN [*to the Old Gentleman*]: Well, what do you think of that?

GROCER [*to the Logician*]: Well, what do you think of that?

GROCER'S WIFE [*to Daisy, from window*]: Well, what do you think of that?

PROPRIETOR [*to the Waitress, who comes back while they are *installing the weeping housewife at one of the terrace tables, still cradling her dead cat*]: A glass of water for the lady.

OLD GENTLEMAN [*to the Housewife*]: Sit down, dear lady!

JEAN: Poor woman!

GROCER'S WIFE [*from window*]: Poor cat!

BERENGER [*to the Waitress*]: Better give her a brandy.

PROPRIETOR [*to the Waitress*]: A brandy! [*Pointing to Berenger*] This gentleman is paying!

WAITRESS [*going into the café*]: One brandy, right away!

HOUSEWIFE [*sobbing*]: I don't want any, I don't want any!

GROCER: It went past my shop a little while ago.

JEAN [*to the Grocer*]: It wasn't the same one!

GROCER [*to Jean*]: But I could have ...

GROCER'S WIFE: Yes it was, it was the same one.

DAISY: Did it go past twice, then?

PROPRIETOR: I think it was the same one.

JEAN: No, it was not the same rhinoceros. The one that went by first had two horns on its nose, it was an Asiatic rhinoceros; this only had one, it was an African rhinoceros!

[*The* WAITRESS *appears with a glass of brandy and takes it to the Housewife.*]

OLD GENTLEMAN: Here's a drop of brandy to pull you together.

HOUSEWIFE [*in tears*]: No ... o ... o ...

BERENGER [*suddenly unnerved, to Jean*]: You're talking nonsense ... How could you possibly tell about the horns? The animal flashed past at such a speed, we hardly even saw it ...

DAISY [*to the Housewife*]: Go on, it will do you good!

OLD GENTLEMAN [*to Berenger*]: Very true. It did go fast.

PROPRIETOR [*to the Housewife*]: Just have a taste, it's good.

BERENGER [*to Jean*]: You had no time to count its horns ...

GROCER'S WIFE [*to the Waitress, from window*]: Make her drink it.

BERENGER [*to Jean*]: What's more, it was travelling in a cloud of dust.

DAISY [*to the Housewife*]: Drink it up.

OLD GENTLEMAN [*to the Housewife*]: Just a sip, dear little lady ... be brave ...
[*The* WAITRESS *forces her to drink it by putting the glass to her lips; the* HOUSEWIFE *feigns refusal, but drinks all the same.*]

WAITRESS: There, you see!

GROCER'S WIFE [*from her window*] *and* DAISY: There, you see!

JEAN [*to Berenger*]: I don't have to grope my way through a fog. I can calculate quickly, my mind is clear!

OLD GENTLEMAN [*to the Housewife*]: Better now?

BERENGER [*to Jean*]: But it had its head thrust down.

PROPRIETOR [*to the Housewife*]: Now wasn't that good?

JEAN [*to Berenger*]: Precisely, one could see all the better.

HOUSEWIFE [*after having drunk*]: My little cat!

BERENGER [*irritated*]: Utter nonsense!

GROCER'S WIFE [*to the Housewife, from window*]: I've got another cat you can have.

JEAN [*to Berenger*]: What me? You dare to accuse me of talking nonsense?

HOUSEWIFE [*to the Grocer's Wife*]: I'll never have another!
[*She weeps, cradling her cat.*]

BERENGER [*to Jean*]: Yes, absolute, blithering nonsense!

PROPRIETOR [*to the Housewife*]: You have to accept these things!

JEAN [*to Berenger*]: I've never talked nonsense in my life!

OLD GENTLEMAN [*to the Housewife*]: Try and be philosophic about it!

BERENGER [*to Jean*]: You're just a pretentious show-off – [*raising his voice*] a pedant!

PROPRIETOR [*to Jean and Berenger*]: Now, gentleman!

BERENGER [*to Jean, continuing*]: ... and what's more, a pedant who's not certain of his facts because in the first place it's the Asiatic rhinoceros with only one horn on its nose, and it's the African with two …

[*The other characters leave the Housewife and crowd round Jean and Berenger who argue at the top of their voices.*]

JEAN [*to Berenger*]: You're wrong, it's the other way about!

HOUSEWIFE [*left alone*]: He was so sweet!

BERENGER: Do you want to bet?

WAITRESS: They want to make a bet!

DAISY [*to Berenger*]: Don't excite yourself, Mr Berenger.

JEAN [*to Berenger*]: I'm not betting with you. If anybody's got two horns, it's you! You Asiatic Mongol!

WAITRESS: Oh!

GROCER'S WIFE [*from window to her husband*]: They're going to have a fight!

GROCER [*to his wife*]: Nonsense, it's just a bet!

PROPRIETOR [*to Jean and Berenger*]: We don't want any scenes here!

OLD GENTLEMAN: Now look … What kind of rhinoceros has one horn on its nose? [*To the Grocer*] You're a tradesman, you should know.

GROCER'S WIFE [*to her husband*]: Yes, you should know!

BERENGER [*to Jean*]: I've got no horns. And I never will have.

GROCER [*to the Old Gentleman*]: Tradesmen can't be expected to know everything.

JEAN [*to Berenger*]: Oh yes, you have!

BERENGER [*to Jean*]: I'm not Asiatic either. And in any case, Asiatics are people the same as everyone else …

WAITRESS: Yes, Asiatics are people the same as we are …

OLD GENTLEMAN [*to the Proprietor*]: That's true!

PROPRIETOR [*to the Waitress*]: Nobody's asking for your opinion!

DAISY [*to the Proprietor*]: She's right. They're people the same as we are.

[*The* HOUSEWIFE *continues to lament throughout this discussion.*]

HOUSEWIFE: He was so gentle, just like one of us.

JEAN [*beside himself*]: They're yellow!

[*The* LOGICIAN, *a little to one side between the Housewife and the group which has formed round Jean and Berenger, follows the controversy attentively, without taking part.*]

Good-bye gentlemen! [*To Berenger*] You, I will not deign to include!

HOUSEWIFE: He was devoted to us! [*She sobs.*]

DAISY: Now listen a moment, Mr Berenger, and you, too, Mr Jean ...

OLD GENTLEMAN: I once had some friends who were Asiatics! But perhaps they weren't real ones ...

PROPRIETOR: I've known some real ones.

WAITRESS [*to the Grocer's Wife*]: I had an Asiatic friend once.

HOUSEWIFE [*still sobbing*]: I had him when he was a little kitten.

JEAN [*still quite beside himself*]: They're yellow, I tell you, bright yellow!

BERENGER [*to Jean*]: Whatever they are, you're bright red!

GROCER'S WIFE [*from window*] *and* WAITRESS: Oh!

PROPRIETOR: This is getting serious!

HOUSEWIFE: He was so clean. He always used his tray.

JEAN [*to Berenger*]: If that's how you feel, it's the last time you'll see me. I'm not wasting my time with a fool like you.

HOUSEWIFE: He always made himself understood.

[JEAN *goes off right, very fast and furious ... but doubles back before making his final exit.*]

OLD GENTLEMAN [*to the Grocer*]: There are white Asiatics as well, and black and blue, and even some like us.

JEAN [*to Berenger*]: You drunkard!

[*Everybody looks at him in consternation.*]

BERENGER [*to Jean*]: I'm not going to stand for that!

ALL [*looking in Jean's direction*]: Oh!

HOUSEWIFE: He could almost talk – in fact he did.

DAISY [*to Berenger*]: You shouldn't have made him angry.

BERENGER [*to Daisy*]: It wasn't my fault.

PROPRIETOR [*to the Waitress*]: Go and get a little coffin for the poor thing ...

OLD GENTLEMAN [*to Berenger*]: I think you're right. It's the Asiatic rhinoceros with two horns and the African with one ...

GROCER: But he was saying the opposite.

DAISY [*to Berenger*]: You were both wrong!

OLD GENTLEMAN [*to Berenger*]: Even so, you were right.

WAITRESS [*to the Housewife*]: Come with me, we're going to put him in a little box.

HOUSEWIFE [*sobbing desperately*]: No, never!

GROCER: If you don't mind my saying so, I think Mr Jean was right.

DAISY [*turning to the Housewife*]: Now, you must be reasonable!

[DAISY *and the* WAITRESS *lead the* HOUSEWIFE, *with her dead cat, towards the café entrance.*]

OLD GENTLEMAN [*to Daisy and the Waitress*]: Would you like me to come with you?

GROCER: The Asiatic rhinoceros has one horn and the African rhinoceros has two. And vice versa.

DAISY [*to the Old Gentleman*]: No, don't you bother.

[DAISY *and the* WAITRESS *enter the café leading the inconsolable* HOUSEWIFE.]

GROCER'S WIFE [*to the Grocer, from window*]: Oh you always have to be different from everybody else!

BERENGER [*aside, whilst the others continue to discuss the horns of the rhinoceros*]: Daisy was right, I should never have contradicted him.

PROPRIETOR [*to the Grocer's Wife*]: Your husband's right, the

Asiatic rhinoceros has two horns and the African one must have two, and vice versa.

BERENGER [aside]: He can't stand being contradicted. The slightest disagreement makes him fume.

OLD GENTLEMAN [to the Proprietor]: You're mistaken, my friend.

PROPRIETOR [to the Old Gentleman]: I'm very sorry, I'm sure.

BERENGER [aside]: His temper's his only fault.

GROCER'S WIFE [from window, to the Old Gentleman, the Proprietor, and the Grocer]: Maybe they're both the same.

BERENGER [aside]: Deep down, he's got a heart of gold; he's done me many a good turn.

PROPRIETOR [to the Grocer's Wife]: If the one has two horns, then the other must have one.

OLD GENTLEMAN: Perhaps it's the other with two and the one with one.

BERENGER [aside]: I'm sorry I wasn't more accommodating. But why is he so obstinate? I didn't want to exasperate him. [To the others] He's always making fantastic statements! Always trying to dazzle people with his knowledge. He never will admit he's wrong.

OLD GENTLEMAN [to Berenger]: Have you any proof?

BERENGER: Proof of what?

OLD GENTLEMAN: Of the statement you made just now which started the unfortunate row with your friend.

GROCER [to Berenger]: Yes, have you any proof?

OLD GENTLEMAN [to Berenger]: How do you know that one of the two rhinoceroses has one horn and the other two? And which is which?

GROCER'S WIFE: He doesn't know any more than we do.

BERENGER: In the first place we don't know that there were two. I myself believe there was only one.

PROPRIETOR: Well, let's say there were two. Does the single-horned one come from Asia?

OLD GENTLEMAN: No. It's the one from Africa with two, I think.

PROPRIETOR: Which is two-horned?

GROCER: It's not the one from Africa.

GROCER'S WIFE: It's not easy to agree on this.

OLD GENTLEMAN: But the problem must be cleared up.

LOGICIAN [*emerging from his isolation*]: Excuse me, gentlemen, for interrupting. But that is not the question. Allow me to introduce myself ...

HOUSEWIFE [*in tears*]: He's a logician.

PROPRIETOR: Oh! A logician, is he?

OLD GENTLEMAN [*introducing the Logician to Berenger*]: My friend, the Logician.

BERENGER: Very happy to meet you.

LOGICIAN [*continuing*]: Professional Logician; my card. [*He shows his card.*]

BERENGER: It's a great honour.

GROCER: A great honour for all of us.

PROPRIETOR: Would you mind telling us then, sir, if the African rhinoceros is single-horned ...

OLD GENTLEMAN: Or bicorned ...

GROCER'S WIFE: And is the Asiatic rhinoceros bicorned ...

GROCER: Or unicorned.

LOGICIAN: Exactly, that is not the question. Let me make myself clear.

GROCER: But it's still what we want to find out.

LOGICIAN: Kindly allow me to speak, gentlemen.

OLD GENTLEMAN: Let him speak!

GROCER'S WIFE [*to the Grocer, from window*]: Give him a chance to speak.

PROPRIETOR: We're listening, sir.

LOGICIAN [*to Berenger*]: I'm addressing you in particular. And all the others present as well.

GROCER: Us as well ...

LOGICIAN: You see, you have got away from the problem which instigated the debate. In the first place you were deliberating whether or not the rhinoceros which passed by just now was the same one that passed by earlier, or whether it was another. That is the question to decide.

BERENGER: Yes, but how?

LOGICIAN: Thus: you may have seen on two occasions a single rhinoceros bearing a single horn ...

GROCER [*repeating the words, as if to understand better*]: On two occasions a single rhinoceros ...

PROPRIETOR [*doing the same*]: Bearing a single horn ...

LOGICIAN: ... or you may have seen on two occasions a single rhinoceros with two horns.

OLD GENTLEMAN [*repeating the words*]: A single rhinoceros with two horns on two occasions ...

LOGICIAN: Exactly. Or again, you may have seen one rhinoceros with one horn, and then another also with a single horn.

GROCER'S WIFE [*from window*]: Ha, ha ...

LOGICIAN: Or again, an initial rhinoceros with two horns, followed by a second with two horns ...

PROPRIETOR: That's true.

LOGICIAN: Now, if you had seen ...

GROCER: If we'd seen ...

OLD GENTLEMAN: Yes, if we'd seen ...

LOGICIAN: If on the first occasion you had seen a rhinoceros with two horns ...

PROPRIETOR: With two horns ...

LOGICIAN: And on the second occasion, a rhinoceros with one horn ...

GROCER: With one horn ...

LOGICIAN: That wouldn't be conclusive either.

OLD GENTLEMAN: Even that wouldn't be conclusive.

PROPRIETOR: Why not?

GROCER'S WIFE: Oh, I don't get it at all.

GROCER: Shoo! Shoo!

[*The* GROCER'S WIFE *shrugs her shoulders and withdraws from her window.*]

LOGICIAN: For it is possible that since its first appearance, the rhinoceros may have lost one of its horns, and that the first and second transit were still made by a single beast.

BERENGER: I see, but ...

OLD GENTLEMAN [*interrupting Berenger*]: Don't interrupt!

LOGICIAN: It may also be that two rhinoceroses both with two horns may each have lost a horn.

OLD GENTLEMAN: That is possible.

PROPRIETOR: Yes, that's possible.

GROCER: Why not?

BERENGER: Yes, but in any case ...

OLD GENTLEMAN [*to Berenger*]: Don't interrupt.

LOGICIAN: If you could prove that on the first occasion you saw a rhinoceros with one horn, either Asiatic or African ...

OLD GENTLEMAN: Asiatic or African ...

LOGICIAN: And on the second occasion a rhinoceros with two horns ...

GROCER: One with two ...

LOGICIAN: No matter whether African or Asiatic ...

OLD GENTLEMAN: African or Asiatic ...

LOGICIAN: ... we could then conclude that we were dealing with two different rhinoceroses, for it is hardly likely that a second horn could grow sufficiently in a space of a few minutes to be visible on the nose of a rhinoceros.

OLD GENTLEMAN: It's hardly likely.

LOGICIAN [*enchanted with his discourse*]: That would imply one rhinoceros either Asiatic or African ...

OLD GENTLEMAN: Asiatic or African ...

LOGICIAN: ... and one rhinoceros either African or Asiatic.

PROPRIETOR: African or Asiatic.

GROCER: Er ... yais.

LOGICIAN: For good logic cannot entertain the possibility that the same creature be born in two places at the same time ...

OLD GENTLEMAN: Or even successively.

LOGICIAN [*to Old Gentleman*]: Which was to be proved.

BERENGER [*to Logician*]: That seems clear enough, but it doesn't answer the question.

LOGICIAN [*to Berenger, with a knowledgeable smile*]: Obviously, my dear sir, but now the problem is correctly posed.

OLD GENTLEMAN: It's quite logical. Quite logical.

LOGICIAN [*raising his hat*]: Good-bye, gentlemen.
[*He retires, going out left, followed by the* OLD GENTLEMAN.]

OLD GENTLEMAN: Good-bye, gentlemen. [*He raises his hat and follows the Logician out.*]

GROCER: Well, it may be logical ...
[*At this moment the* HOUSEWIFE *comes out of the café in deep mourning, and carrying a box; she is followed by* DAISY *and the* WAITRESS *as if for a funeral. The cortège moves towards the right exit.*]
... it may be logical, but are we going to stand for our cats being run down under our very eyes by one-horned rhinoceroses or two, whether they're Asiatic or African? [*He indicates with a theatrical gesture the cortège which is just leaving.*]

PROPRIETOR: He's absolutely right! We're not standing for our cats being run down by rhinoceroses or anything else!

GROCER: We're not going to stand for it!

GROCER'S WIFE [*sticking her head round the shop door, to her husband*]: Are you coming in? The customers will be here any minute.

GROCER [*moving to the shop*]: No, we're not standing for it.

BERENGER: I should never have quarrelled with Jean! [*To the Proprietor*] Get me a brandy! A double!

PROPRIETOR: Coming up! [*He goes into the café for the brandy.*]

BERENGER [*alone*]: I never should have quarrelled with Jean. I shouldn't have got into such a rage!

[*The Proprietor comes out carrying a large glass of brandy.*]

I feel too upset to go to the museum. I'll cultivate my mind some other time. [*He takes the glass of brandy and drinks it.*]

CURTAIN

ACT TWO

SCENE ONE

A government office, or the office of a private concern – such as a large firm of law publications. Up-stage centre, a large double door, above which a notice reads: 'Chef du Service.' Up-stage left, near to the Head of the Department's door, stands Daisy's little table with a typewriter. By the left wall, between a door which leads to the stair-case and Daisy's table, stands another table on which the time sheets are placed, which the employees sign on arrival. The door leading to the staircase is down-stage left. The top steps of the staircase can be seen, the top of a stair-rail and a small landing. In the foreground, a table with two chairs. On the table: printing proofs, an inkwell, pens; this is the table where Botard and Berenger work; Berenger will sit on the left chair, Botard on the right. Near to the right wall, another bigger, rectangular table, also covered with papers, proofs, etc.

Two more chairs stand at each end of this table – more elegant and imposing chairs. This is the table of Dudard and Mr Boeuf. Dudard will sit on the chair next to the wall, the other employees facing him. He acts as Deputy-Head. Between the up-stage door and the right wall, there is a window. If the theatre has an orchestra pit it would be preferable to have simply a window frame in front of the stage, facing the auditorium. In the right-hand corner, up-stage, a coat-stand, on which grey blouses or old coats are hung. The coat-stand could also be placed down-stage, near to the right wall.

On the walls are rows of books and dusty documents. On the back wall, left, above the shelves, there are signs: 'Jurisprudence', 'Codes'; on the right-hand wall which can be slightly on an angle, the signs read: 'Le Journal Officiel', 'Lois fiscales'. Above the

*Head of the Department's door a clock registers three minutes past
nine.*

When the curtain rises, DUDARD *is standing near his chair, his
right profile to the auditorium; on the other side of the desk, left profile to the auditorium, is* BOTARD; *between them, also near to the
desk, facing the auditorium, stands the Head of the Department;*
DAISY *is near to the Chief, a little up-stage of him. She holds some
sheets of typing paper. On the table round which the three characters
stand, a large open newspaper lies on the printing proofs.*

*When the curtain rises the characters remain fixed for a few seconds
in position for the first line of dialogue. They make a tableau vivant.
The same effect marks the beginning of the first act.*

*The Head of the Department is about forty, very correctly dressed:
dark blue suit, a rosette of the Legion of Honour, starched collar,
black tie, large brown moustache. He is Mr Papillon.*

*Dudard, thirty-five years old; grey suit; he wears black lustrine
sleeves to protect his coat. He may wear spectacles. He is a quite tall,
young employee with a future. If the Department Head became the
Assistant Director he would take his place: Botard does not like him.*

*Botard: former schoolteacher; short, he has a proud air, and wears a
little white moustache; a brisk sixty-year-old (he knows everything,
understands everything, judges everything). He wears a Basque
beret, and wears a long grey blouse during working hours; spectacles
on a longish nose; a pencil behind his ear; he also wears protective
sleeves at work.*

Daisy: a young blonde.

*Later, Mrs Boeuf; a large woman of some forty to fifty years old,
tearful and breathless.*

> [*As the curtain rises, the characters therefore are standing
> motionless around the table, right; the Chief with index finger
> pointing to the newspaper;* DUDARD, *with his hand extended
> in* BOTARD'S *direction, seems to be saying: 'so you see!'*
> BOTARD, *hands in the pocket of his blouse, wears an in-
> credulous smile and seems to say: 'You won't take me in.'*

DAISY, *with her typing paper in her hand, seems, from her look, to be supporting Dudard.*

After a few brief seconds, BOTARD *starts the attack.*]

BOTARD: It's all a lot of made-up nonsense.

DAISY: But I saw it, I saw the rhinoceros!

DUDARD: It's in the paper, in black and white, you can't deny that.

BOTARD [*with an air of the greatest scorn*]: Pfff!

DUDARD: It's all here; it's down here in the dead cats column! Read it for yourself, Chief.

PAPILLON: 'Yesterday, just before lunch time, in the church square of our town, a cat was trampled to death by a pachyderm.'

DAISY: It wasn't exactly in the church square.

PAPILLON: That's all it says. No other details.

BOTARD: Pfff!

DUDARD: Well, that's clear enough.

BOTARD: I never believe journalists. They're all liars. I don't need them to tell me what to think; I believe what I see with my own eyes. Speaking as a former teacher, I like things to be precise, scientifically valid; I've got a methodical mind.

DUDARD: What's a methodical mind got to do with it?

DAISY [*to Botard*]: I think it's stated very precisely, Mr Botard.

BOTARD: You call that precise? And what, pray, does it mean by a pachyderm? What does the editor of a dead cats column understand by a pachyderm? He doesn't say. And what does he mean by a cat?

DUDARD: Everybody knows what a cat is.

BOTARD: Does it concern a male cat or a female? What breed was it? And what colour? The colour bar is something I feel strongly about. I hate it.

PAPILLON: What has the colour bar to do with it, Mr Botard? It's quite beside the point.

BOTARD: Please forgive me, Mr Papillon. But you can't deny

49

that the colour problem is one of the great stumbling blocks of our time.

DUDARD: I know that, we all know that, but it has nothing to do with ...

BOTARD: It's not an issue to be dismissed lightly, Mr Dudard. The course of history has shown that racial prejudice ...

DUDARD: I tell you it doesn't enter into it.

BOTARD: I'm not so sure.

PAPILLON: The colour bar is not the issue at stake.

BOTARD: One should never miss an occasion to denounce it.

DAISY: But we told you that none of us is in favour of the colour bar. You're obscuring the issue; it's simply a question of a cat being run over by a pachyderm – in this case, a rhinoceros.

BOTARD: I'm a Northerner myself. Southerners have got too much imagination. Perhaps it was merely a flea run over by a mouse. People make mountains out of molehills.

PAPILLON [to Dudard]: Let us try and get things clear. Did you yourself, with your own eyes, see a rhinoceros strolling through the streets of the town?

DAISY: It didn't stroll, it ran.

DUDARD: No, I didn't see it personally. But a lot of very reliable people ...!

BOTARD [interrupting him]: It's obvious they were just making it up. You put too much trust in these journalists; they don't care what they invent to sell their wretched newspapers and please the bosses they serve! And you mean to tell me they've taken you in – you, a qualified man of law! Forgive me for laughing! Ha! Ha! Ha!

DAISY: But I saw it, I saw the rhinoceros. I'd take my oath on it.

BOTARD: Get away with you! And I thought you were a sensible girl!

DAISY: Mr Botard, I can see straight! And I wasn't the only one; there were plenty of other people watching.

BOTARD: Pfff! They were probably watching something else! A few idlers with nothing to do, work-shy loafers!

DUDARD: It happened yesterday, Sunday.

BOTARD: I work on Sundays as well. I've no time for priests who do their utmost to get you to church, just to prevent you from working, and earning your daily bread by the sweat of your brow.

PAPILLON [*indignant*]: Oh!

BOTARD: I'm sorry, I didn't mean to offend you. The fact that I despise religion doesn't mean I don't esteem it highly. [*To Daisy*] In any case, do you know what a rhinoceros looks like?

DAISY: It's a ... it's a very big ugly animal.

BOTARD: And you pride yourself on your precise thinking! The rhinoceros, my dear young lady ...

PAPILLON: There's no need to start a lecture on the rhinoceros here. We're not in school.

BOTARD: That's a pity.

[*During these last speeches* BERENGER *is seen climbing the last steps of the staircase; he opens the office door cautiously; as he does so one can read the notice on it:* 'Éditions de Droit.']

PAPILLON: Well! It's gone nine, Miss Daisy; put the time sheets away. Too bad about the late-comers.

[DAISY *goes to the little table, left, on which the time sheets are placed, at the same moment as* BERENGER *enters.*]

BERENGER [*entering, whilst the others continue their discussion, to Daisy*]: Good morning, Miss Daisy. I'm not late, am I?

BOTARD: [*to Dudard and Papillon*]: I campaign against ignorance wherever I find it ...!

DAISY [*to Berenger*]: Hurry up, Mr Berenger.

BOTARD: ... in palace or humble hut!

DAISY [*to Berenger*]: Quick! Sign the time sheet!

BERENGER: Oh thank you! Has the Boss arrived?

DAISY [*a finger on her lips*]: Shh! Yes, he's here.

BERENGER: Here already? [*He hurries to sign the time sheet.*]

BOTARD [*continuing*]: No matter where! Even in printing offices.

PAPILLON [*to Botard*]: Mr Botard, I consider ...

BERENGER [*signing the sheet, to Daisy*]: But it's not ten past ...

PAPILLON [*to Botard*]: I consider you have gone too far.

DUDARD [*to Papillon*]: I think so too, sir.

PAPILLON [*to Botard*]: Are you suggesting that Mr Dudard, my colleague and yours, a law graduate and a first-class employee, is ignorant?

BOTARD: I wouldn't go so far as to say that, but the teaching you get at the university isn't up to what you get at the ordinary schools.

PAPILLON [*to Daisy*]: What about that time sheet?

DAISY [*to Papillon*]: Here it is, sir. [*She hands it to him.*]

BOTARD [*to Dudard*]: There's no clear thinking at the universities, no encouragement for practical observation.

DUDARD [*to Botard*]: Oh come now!

BERENGER [*to Papillon*]: Good morning, Mr Papillon. [*He has been making his way to the coat-rack behind the Chief's back and around the group formed by the three characters; there he takes down his working overall or his well-worn coat, and hangs up his street coat in its place; he changes his coat by the coat-rack, then makes his way to his desk, from the drawer of which he takes out his black protective sleeves, etc.*] Morning, Mr Papillon! Sorry I was almost late. Morning, Dudard! Morning, Mr Botard.

PAPILLON: Well, Berenger, did you see the rhinoceros by any chance?

BOTARD [*to Dudard*]: All you get at the universities are effete intellectuals with no practical knowledge of life.

DUDARD [*to Botard*]: Rubbish!

BERENGER [*continuing to arrange his working equipment with excessive zeal as if to make up for his late arrival; in a natural tone to Papillon*]: Oh yes, I saw it all right.

BOTARD [*turning round*]: Pfff!

DAISY: So you see, I'm not mad after all.

BOTARD [*ironic*]: Oh, Mr Berenger says that out of chivalry –
he's a very chivalrous man even if he doesn't look it.

DUDARD: What's chivalrous about saying you've seen a
rhinoceros?

BOTARD: A lot – when it's said to bolster up a fantastic statement by Miss Daisy. Everybody is chivalrous to Miss Daisy,
it's very understandable.

PAPILLON: Don't twist the facts, Mr Botard. Mr Berenger
took no part in the argument. He's only just arrived.

BERENGER [*to Daisy*]: But you did see it, didn't you? We both
did.

BOTARD: Pfff! It's possible that Mr Berenger thought he saw
a rhinoceros. [*He makes a sign behind Berenger's back to indi-
cate he drinks.*] He's got such a vivid imagination! Anything's
possible with him!

BERENGER: I wasn't alone when I saw the rhinoceros! Or perhaps there were two rhinoceroses.

BOTARD: He doesn't even know how many he saw.

BERENGER: I was with my friend Jean! And other people were
there, too.

BOTARD [*to Berenger*]: I don't think you know what you're
talking about.

DAISY: It was a unicorned rhinoceros.

BOTARD: Pff! They're in league, the two of them, to have us
on.

DUDARD [*to Daisy*]: I rather think it had two horns, from
what I've heard!

BOTARD: You'd better make up your minds.

PAPILLON [*looking at the time*]: That will do, gentlemen, time's
getting on.

BOTARD: Did you see one rhinoceros, Mr Berenger, or two
rhinoceroses?

BERENGER: Well, it's hard to say!

BOTARD: You don't know. Miss Daisy saw one unicorned rhinoceros. What about your rhinoceros, Mr Berenger, if indeed there was one, did it have one horn or two?

BERENGER: Exactly, that's the whole problem.

BOTARD: And it's all very dubious.

DAISY: Oh!

BOTARD: I don't mean to be offensive. But I don't believe a word of it. No rhinoceros has ever been seen in this country!

DAISY: There's a first time for everything.

BOTARD: It has never been seen! Except in school-book illustrations. Your rhinoceroses are a flower of some washerwoman's imagination.

BERENGER: The word 'flower' applied to a rhinoceros seems a bit out of place.

DUDARD: Very true.

BOTARD [continuing]: Your rhinoceros is a myth!

DAISY: A myth?

PAPILLON: Gentlemen, I think it is high time we started to work.

BOTARD [to Daisy]: A myth – like flying saucers.

DUDARD: But nevertheless a cat was trampled to death – that you can't deny.

BERENGER: I was a witness to that.

DUDARD [pointing to Berenger]: In front of witnesses.

BOTARD: Yes, and what a witness!

PAPILLON: Gentlemen, gentlemen!

BOTARD [to Dudard]: An example of collective psychosis, Mr Dudard. Just like religion – the opiate of the people!

DAISY: Well I believe flying saucers exist!

BOTARD: Pfff!

PAPILLON [firmly]: That's quite enough. There's been enough gossip! Rhinoceros or no rhinoceros, saucers or no saucers, work must go on! You're not paid to waste your time arguing about real or imaginary animals.

BOTARD: Imaginary!

DUDARD: Real!

DAISY: Very real!

PAPILLON: Gentlemen, I remind you once again that we are in working hours. I am putting an end to this futile discussion.

BOTARD [*wounded and ironic*]: Very well, Mr Papillon. You are the Chief. Your wishes are our commands.

PAPILLON: Get on, gentlemen. I don't want to be forced to make a deduction from your salaries! Mr Dudard, how is your report on the alcoholic repression law coming along?

DUDARD: I'm just finishing it off, sir.

PAPILLON: Then do so. It's very urgent. Mr Berenger and Mr Botard, have you finished correcting the proofs for the wine trade control regulations?

BERENGER: Not yet, Mr Papillon. But they're well on the way.

PAPILLON: Then finish off the corrections together. The printers are waiting. And Miss Daisy, you bring the letters to my office for signature. Hurry up and get them typed.

DAISY: Very good, Mr Papillon.

[DAISY *goes and types at her little desk.* DUDARD *sits at his desk and starts to work.* BERENGER *and* BOTARD *sit at their little tables in profile to the auditorium.* BOTARD, *his back to the staircase, seems in a bad temper.* BERENGER *is passive and limp; he spreads the proofs on the table, passes the manuscript to* BOTARD; BOTARD *sits down grumbling, whilst* PAPILLON *exits banging the door loudly.*]

PAPILLON: I shall see you shortly, gentlemen. [*Goes out.*]

BERENGER [*reading and correcting whilst* BOTARD *checks the manuscript with a pencil*]: Laws relating to the control of pro-prietary wine produce ... [*He corrects.*] control with one L ...

[*He corrects.*] proprietary ... one P, proprietary ... The controlled wines of the Bordeaux region, the lower sections of the upper slopes ...

BOTARD: I haven't got that! You've skipped a line.

BERENGER: I'll start again. The Wine Control!

DUDARD [*to Berenger and Botard*]: Please don't read so loud. I can't concentrate with you shouting at the tops of your voices.

BOTARD [*to Dudard, over Berenger's head, resuming the recent discussion, whilst Berenger continues the corrections on his own for a few moments; he moves his lips noiselessly as he reads*]: It's all a hoax.

DUDARD: What's all a hoax?

BOTARD: Your rhinoceros business, of course. You've been making all this propaganda to get these rumours started!

DUDARD [*interrupting his work*]: What propaganda?

BERENGER [*breaking in*]: No question of any propaganda.

DAISY [*interrupting her typing*]: Do I have to tell you again, I saw it ... I actually saw it, and others did, too.

DUDARD [*to Botard*]: You make me laugh! Propaganda! Propaganda for what?

BOTARD [*to Dudard*]: Oh you know more about that than I do. Don't make out you're so innocent.

DUDARD [*getting angry*]: At any rate, Mr Botard, I'm not in the pay of any furtive underground organization.

BOTARD: That's an insult, I'm not standing for that ... [*Rises.*]

BERENGER [*pleading*]: Now, now, Mr Botard ...

DAISY [*to Dudard, who has also risen*]: Now, now, Mr Dudard ...

BOTARD: I tell you it's an insult.

[*Mr Papillon's door suddenly opens.* BOTARD *and* DUDARD *sit down again quickly;* MR PAPILLON *is holding the time sheet in his hand; there is silence at his appearance.*]

PAPILLON: Is Mr Boeuf not in today?

BERENGER [*looking around*]: No, he isn't. He must be absent.

PAPILLON: Just when I needed him. [*To Daisy*] Did he let anyone know he was ill or couldn't come in?

DAISY: He didn't say anything to me.

PAPILLON [*opening his door wide, and coming in*]: If this goes on I shall fire him. It's not the first time he's played me this trick. Up to now I haven't said anything, but it's not going on like this. Has anyone got the key to his desk?

[*At this moment* MRS BOEUF *enters. She has been seen during the last speech coming up the stairs. She bursts through the door, out of breath, apprehensive.*]

BERENGER: Oh here's Mrs Boeuf.

DAISY: Morning, Mrs Boeuf.

MRS BOEUF: Morning, Mr Papillon. Good morning, everyone.

PAPILLON: Well, where's your husband? What's happened to him? Is it too much trouble for him to come any more?

MRS BOEUF [*breathless*]: Please excuse him, my husband I mean ... he went to visit his family for the week-end. He's got a touch of flu.

PAPILLON: So he's got a touch of flu, has he?

MRS BOEUF [*handing a paper to Papillon*]: He says so in the telegram. He hopes to be back on Wednesday ... [*Almost fainting*] Could I have a glass of water ... and sit down a moment ...

[BERENGER *takes his own chair centre-stage, on which she flops.*]

PAPILLON [*to Daisy*]: Give her a glass of water.

DAISY: Yes, straightaway! [*She goes to get her a glass of water, and gives it to her during the following speeches.*]

DUDARD [*to Papillon*]: She must have a weak heart.

PAPILLON: It's a great nuisance that Mr Boeuf can't come. But that's no reason for you to go to pieces.

MRS BOEUF [*with difficulty*]: It's not ... it's ... well I was chased here all the way from the house by a rhinoceros ...

BERENGER: How many horns did it have?

BOTARD [*guffawing*]: Don't make me laugh!

DUDARD [*indignant*]: Give her a chance to speak!

MRS BOEUF [*making a great effort to be exact, and pointing in the direction of the staircase*]: It's down there, by the entrance. It seemed to want to come upstairs.

[*At this moment a noise is heard. The staircase steps are seen to crumble under an obviously formidable weight. From below an anguished trumpeting is heard. As the dust clears after the collapse of the staircase, the staircase landing is seen to be hanging in space.*]

DAISY: My God!

MRS BOEUF [*seated, her hand on her heart*]: Oh! Ah!

[BERENGER *runs to administer to Mrs Boeuf, patting her cheeks and making her drink.*]

BERENGER: Keep calm!

[*Meanwhile* PAPILLON, DUDARD, *and* BOTARD *rush left, jostling each other in their efforts to open the door, and stand covered in dust on the landing; the trumpetings continue to be heard.*]

DAISY [*to Mrs Boeuf*]: Are you feeling better now, Mrs Boeuf?

PAPILLON [*on the landing*]: There it is! Down there! It is one!

BOTARD: I can't see a thing. It's an illusion.

DUDARD: Of course it's one, down there, turning round and round.

PAPILLON: No doubt about it, gentlemen – it's turning round and round.

DUDARD: It can't get up here. There's no staircase any longer.

BOTARD: It's most strange. What can it mean?

DUDARD [*turning towards Berenger*]: Come and look. Come and have a look at your rhinoceros.

BERENGER: I'm coming.

[BERENGER *rushes to the landing, followed by* DAISY *who abandons Mrs Boeuf.*]

PAPILLON [*to Berenger*]: You're the rhinoceros expert – take a good look.

BERENGER: I'm no rhinoceros expert ...

DAISY: Oh look at the way it's going round and round. It looks as if it was in pain ... what can it want?

DUDARD: It seems to be looking for someone. [*To Botard*] Can you see it now?

BOTARD [*vexed*]: Yes, yes, I can see it.

DAISY [*to Papillon*]: Perhaps we're all seeing things. You as well ...

BOTARD: I never see things. Something is definitely down there.

DUDARD [*to Botard*]: What do you mean, something?

PAPILLON [*to Berenger*]: It's obviously a rhinoceros. That's what you saw before, isn't it? [*To Daisy*] And you, too?

DAISY: Definitely.

BERENGER: It's got two horns. It's an African rhinoceros, or Asiatic rather. Oh! I don't know whether the African rhinoceros has one horn or two.

PAPILLON: It's demolished the staircase – and a good thing, too! When you think how long I've been asking the management to install stone steps in place of that worm-eaten old staircase.

DUDARD: I sent a report a week ago, Chief.

PAPILLON: It was bound to happen, I knew that. I could see it coming, and I was right.

DAISY [*to Papillon, ironically*]: As always.

BERENGER [*to Dudard and Papillon*]: Now look, are two horns a characteristic of the Asiatic rhinoceros or the African? And is one horn a characteristic of the African or the Asiatic one ... ?

DAISY: Poor thing, it keeps on trumpeting and going round

and round. What does it want? Oh, it's looking at us! [*To the rhinoceros*] Puss, puss, puss ...

DUDARD: I shouldn't try to stroke it, it's probably not tame ...

PAPILLON: In any case, it's out of reach.

[*The rhinoceros gives a horrible trumpeting.*]

DAISY: Poor thing!

BERENGER [*to Botard, still insisting*]: You're very well informed, don't you think that the ones with two horns are ...

PAPILLON: What are you rambling on about, Berenger? You're still a bit under the weather, Mr Botard was right.

BOTARD: How can it be possible in a civilized country ...?

DAISY [*to Botard*]: All right. But does it exist or not?

BOTARD: It's all an infamous plot! [*With a political orator's gesture he points to Dudard, quelling him with a look.*] It's all your fault!

DUDARD: Why mine, rather than yours?

BOTARD [*furious*]: Mine? It's always the little people who get the blame. If I had my way ...

PAPILLON: We're in a fine mess with no staircase.

DAISY [*to Botard and Dudard*]: Calm down, this is no time to quarrel!

PAPILLON: It's all the management's fault.

DAISY: Maybe. But how are we going to get down?

PAPILLON [*joking amorously and caressing Daisy's cheek*]: I'll take you in my arms and we'll float down together.

DAISY [*rejecting Papillon's advances*]: You keep your horny hands off my face, you old pachyderm!

PAPILLON: I was only joking!

[*Meanwhile the rhinoceros has continued its trumpeting.* MRS BOEUF *has risen and joined the group. For a few moments she stares fixedly at the rhinoceros turning round and round below; suddenly she lets out a terrible cry.*]

MRS BOEUF: My God! It can't be true!

BERENGER [*to Mrs Boeuf*]: What's the matter?

MRS BOEUF: It's my husband. Oh Boeuf, my poor Boeuf, what's happened to you?

DAISY [to Mrs Boeuf]: Are you positive?

MRS BOEUF: I recognize him, I recognize him!

[The rhinoceros replies with a violent but tender trumpeting.]

PAPILLON: Well! That's the last straw. This time he's fired for good!

DUDARD: Is he insured?

BOTARD [aside]: I understand it all now ...

DAISY: How can you collect insurance in a case like this?

MRS BOEUF [fainting into Berenger's arms]: Oh! My God!

BERENGER: Oh!

DAISY: Carry her over here!

[BERENGER, helped by DUDARD and DAISY, installs MRS BOEUF in a chair.]

DUDARD [while they are carrying her]: Don't upset yourself, Mrs Boeuf.

MRS BOEUF: Ah! Oh!

DAISY: Maybe it can all be put right ...

PAPILLON [to Dudard]: Legally, what can be done?

DUDARD: You need to get a solicitor's advice.

BOTARD [following the procession, raising his hands to heaven]: It's the sheerest madness! What a society!

[They crowd round MRS BOEUF, pinching her cheeks; she opens her eyes, emits an 'Ah' and closes them again; they continue to pinch her cheeks as BOTARD speaks.]

You can be certain of one thing: I shall report this to my union. I don't desert a colleague in the hour of need. It won't be hushed up.

MRS BOEUF [coming to]: My poor darling, I can't leave him like that, my poor darling. [A trumpeting is heard.] He's calling me. [Tenderly] He's calling me.

DAISY: Feeling better now, Mrs Boeuf?

DUDARD: She's picking up a bit.

BOTARD [*to Mrs Boeuf*]: You can count on the union's support. Would you like to become a member of the committee?

PAPILLON: Work's going to be delayed again. What about the post, Miss Daisy?

DAISY: I want to know first how we're going to get out of here.

PAPILLON: It is a problem. Through the window.

[*They all go to the window with the exception of* MRS BOEUF *slumped in her chair and* BOTARD *who stays centre-stage.*]

BOTARD: I know where it came from.

DAISY [*at window*]: It's too high.

BERENGER: Perhaps we ought to call the firemen, and get them to bring ladders!

PAPILLON: Miss Daisy, go to my office and telephone the fire brigade. [*He makes as if to follow her.*]

[DAISY *goes out up-stage and one hears her voice on the telephone say:* 'Hello, hello, is that the Fire Brigade?' *followed by a vague sound of telephone conversation.*]

MRS BOEUF [*rising suddenly*]: I can't desert him, I can't desert him now!

PAPILLON: If you want to divorce him ... you'd be perfectly justified.

DUDARD: You'd be the injured party.

MRS BOEUF: No! Poor thing! This is not the moment for that. I won't abandon my husband in such a state.

BOTARD: You're a good woman.

DUDARD [*to Mrs Boeuf*]: But what are you going to do?

[*She runs left towards the landing.*]

BERENGER: Watch out!

MRS BOEUF: I can't leave him, I can't leave him now!

DUDARD: Hold her back!

MRS BOEUF: I'm taking him home!

PAPILLON: What's she trying to do?

MRS BOEUF [*preparing to jump; on the edge of the landing*]: I'm coming, my darling, I'm coming!

BERENGER: She's going to jump.

BOTARD: It's no more than her duty.

DUDARD: She can't do that.

[*Everyone with the exception of* DAISY, *who is still telephoning, is near to* MRS BOEUF *on the landing; she jumps;* BERENGER, *who tries to restrain her, is left with her skirt in his hand.*]

BERENGER: I couldn't hold her back.

[*The rhinoceros is heard from below, tenderly trumpeting.*]

VOICE OF MRS BOEUF: Here I am, my sweet, I'm here now.

DUDARD: She landed on his back in the saddle.

BOTARD: She's a good rider.

VOICE OF MRS BOEUF: Home now, dear, let's go home.

DUDARD: They're off at a gallop.

[DUDARD, BOTARD, BERENGER, PAPILLON *come back on-stage and go to the window.*]

BERENGER: They're moving fast.

DUDARD [*to Papillon*]: Ever done any riding?

PAPILLON: A bit ... a long time ago ... [*Turning to the up-stage door, to Dudard*] Is she still on the telephone?

BERENGER [*following the course of the rhinoceros*]: They're already a long way off. They're out of sight.

DAISY [*coming on-stage*]: I had trouble getting the firemen.

BOTARD [*as if concluding an interior monologue*]: A fine state of affairs!

DAISY: ... I had trouble getting the firemen!

PAPILLON: Are there fires all over the place, then?

BERENGER: I agree with Mr Botard. Mrs Boeuf's attitude is very moving; she's a woman of feeling.

PAPILLON: It means one employee less, who has to be replaced.

BERENGER: Do you really think he's no use to us any more?

DAISY: No, there aren't any fires, the firemen have been called out for other rhinoceroses.

BERENGER: For other rhinoceroses?

DAISY: Yes, other rhinoceroses. They've been reported all

over the town. This morning there were seven, now there are seventeen.

BOTARD: What did I tell you?

DAISY: As many as thirty-two have been reported. They're not official yet, but they're bound to be confirmed soon.

BOTARD [less certain]: Pff! They always exaggerate.

PAPILLON: Are they coming to get us out of here?

BERENGER: I'm hungry ...!

DAISY: Yes, they're coming; the firemen are on the way.

PAPILLON: What about the work?

DUDARD: It looks as if it's out of our hands.

PAPILLON: We'll have to make up the lost time.

DUDARD: Well, Mr Botard, do you still deny all rhinocerotic evidence?

BOTARD: Our union is against your dismissing Mr Boeuf without notice.

PAPILLON: It's not up to me; we shall see what conclusions they reach at the inquiry.

BOTARD [to Dudard]: No, Mr Dudard, I do not deny the rhinocerotic evidence. I never have.

DUDARD: That's not true.

DAISY: Oh no, that's not true.

BOTARD: I repeat I have never denied it. I just wanted to find out exactly where it was all leading. Because I know my own mind. I'm not content to simply state that a phenomenon exists. I make it my business to understand and explain it. At least I could explain it if ...

DUDARD: Then explain it to us.

DAISY: Yes, explain it, Mr Botard.

PAPILLON: Explain it, when your colleagues ask you.

BOTARD: I will explain it ...

DUDARD: We're all listening.

DAISY: I'm most curious.

BOTARD: I will expalin it ... one day ...

DUDARD: Why not now?

BOTARD [*menacingly; to Mr Papillon*]: We'll go into the explanation later, in private. [*To everyone*] I know the whys and the wherefores of this whole business ...

DAISY: What whys?

BERENGER: What wherefores?

DUDARD: I'd give a lot to know these whys and wherefores ...

BOTARD [*continuing; with a terrible air*]: And I also know the names of those responsible. The names of the traitors. You can't fool me. I'll let you know the purpose and the meaning of this whole plot! I'll unmask the perpetrators!

BERENGER: But who'd want to ...

DUDARD [*to Botard*]: You're evading the question, Mr Botard.

PAPILLON: Let's have no evasions.

BOTARD: Evading? What, me?

DAISY: Just now you accused us of suffering from hallucinations.

BOTARD: Just now, yes. Now the hallucination has become a provocation.

DUDARD: And how do you consider this change came about?

BOTARD: It's an open secret, gentlemen. Even the man in the street knows about it. Only hypocrites pretend not to understand.

[*The noise and hooting of a fire-engine is heard. The brakes are abruptly applied just under the window.*]

DAISY: That's the firemen!

BOTARD: There're going to be some big changes made; they won't get away with it as easily as that.

DUDARD: That doesn't mean anything, Mr Botard. The rhinoceroses exist, and that's that. That's all there is to it.

DAISY [*at the window, looking down*]: Up here, firemen!

[*A bustling is heard below, commotion, engine noises.*]

VOICE OF FIREMAN: Put up the ladder!

65

BOTARD [*to Dudard*]: I hold the key to all these happenings, an infallible system of interpretation.

PAPILLON: I want you all back in the office this afternoon.

[*The firemen's ladder is placed against the window.*]

BOTARD: Too bad about the office, Mr Papillon.

PAPILLON: I don't know what the management will say!

DUDARD: These are exceptional circumstances.

BOTARD [*pointing to the window*]: They can't force us to come back this way. We'll have to wait till the staircase is repaired.

DUDARD: If anyone breaks a leg, it'll be the management's responsibility.

PAPILLON: That's true.

[*A fireman's helmet is seen, followed by the fireman.*]

BERENGER [*to Daisy, pointing to the window*]: After you, Miss Daisy.

FIREMAN: Come on, Miss.

[*The fireman takes Daisy in his arms; she steps astride the window and disappears with him.*]

DUDARD: Good-bye, Miss Daisy. See you soon.

DAISY [*disappearing*]: See you soon, good-bye!

PAPILLON [*at window*]: Telephone me tomorrow morning, Miss Daisy. You can come and type the letters at my house. [*To Berenger*] Mr Berenger, I draw your attention to the fact that we are not on holiday, and that work will resume as soon as possible. [*To the other two*] You hear what I say, gentlemen?

DUDARD: Of course, Mr Papillon.

BOTARD: They'll go on exploiting us till we drop, of course.

FIREMAN [*reappearing at window*]: Who's next?

PAPILLON [*to all three of them*]: Go on!

DUDARD: After you, Mr Papillon.

BERENGER: After you, Chief.

BOTARD: You first, of course.

PAPILLON [*to Berenger*]: Bring me Miss Daisy's letters. There, on the table.

[BERENGER *goes and gets the letters, brings them to Papillon.*]

FIREMAN: Come on, hurry up. We've not got all day. We've got other calls to make.

BOTARD: What did I tell you?

[PAPILLON, *the letters under his arm, steps astride the window.*]

PAPILLON [*to the Fireman*]: Careful of the documents! [*Turning to the others*]: Good-bye, gentlemen.

DUDARD: Good-bye, Mr Papillon.

BERENGER: Good-bye, Mr Papillon.

PAPILLON [*he has disappeared; one hears him say*]: Careful of my papers. Dudard! Lock up the offices!

DUDARD [*shouting*]: Don't you worry, Mr Papillon. [*To Botard*] After you, Mr Botard.

BOTARD: I am about to descend, gentlemen. And I am going to take this matter up immediately with the proper authorities. I'll get to the bottom of this so-called mystery. [*He moves to the window.*]

DUDARD [*to Botard*]: I thought it was all perfectly clear to you!

BOTARD [*astride the window*]: Your irony doesn't affect me. What I'm after are the proofs and the documents – yes, proof positive of your treason.

DUDARD: That's absurd ...

BOTARD: Your insults ...

DUDARD [*interrupting him*]: It's you who are insulting me ...

BOTARD [*disappearing*]: I don't insult. I merely prove.

VOICE OF FIREMAN: Come on there!

DUDARD [*to Berenger*]: What are you doing this afternoon? Shall we meet for a drink?

BERENGER: Sorry I can't. I'm taking advantage of this afternoon off to go and see my friend Jean. I do want to make it up with him, after all. We got carried away. It was all my fault.

[*The fireman's head reappears at the window.*]

FIREMAN: Come along there!

BERENGER [*pointing to the window*]: After you.

DUDARD: After you.

BERENGER: Oh no, after you.

DUDARD: No, I insist, after you.

BERENGER: No, please, after you, after you.

FIREMAN: Hurry up!

DUDARD: After you, after you.

BERENGER: No, after you, after you.

[*They climb through the window together. The fireman helps them down, as the curtain falls.*]

CURTAIN

SCENE TWO

Jean's house. The layout is roughly the same as Act Two, Scene One. That is to say, the stage is divided into two. To the right, occupying three-quarters or four-fifths of the stage, according to its size, is Jean's bedroom. Up-stage, a chair or an armchair, on which Berenger will sit. Right centre, a door leading to Jean's bathroom. When Jean goes in to wash, the noise of a tap is heard, and that of the shower. To the left of the room, a partition divides the stage in two. Centre-stage, the door leading to the stairs. If a less realistic, more stylized décor is preferred, the door may be placed without a partition. To the left is the staircase; the top steps are visible, leading to

Jean's flat, the banister, and the landing. At the back, on the landing level, is the door to the neighbour's flat. Lower down, at the back, there is a glass door, over which is written: 'Concierge.'

[*When the curtain rises,* JEAN *is in bed, lying under the blanket, his back to the audience. One hears him cough.*

After a few moments BERENGER *is seen, climbing the top steps of the staircase. He knocks at the door;* JEAN *does not answer.* BERENGER *knocks again.*]

BERENGER: Jean! [*He knocks again.*] Jean!

[*The door at the end of the landing opens slightly, and a little old man with a white goatee appears.*]

OLD MAN: What is it?

BERENGER: I want to see Jean. I am a friend of his.

OLD MAN: I thought it was me you wanted. My name's Jean as well, but it's the other one you want.

VOICE OF OLD MAN'S WIFE [*from within the room*]: Is it for us?

OLD MAN [*turning to his wife who is not seen*]: No, for the other one.

BERENGER [*knocking*]: Jean!

OLD MAN: I didn't see him go out. But I saw him last night. He looked in a bad temper.

BERENGER: Yes, I know why; it was my fault.

OLD MAN: Perhaps he doesn't feel like opening the door to you. Try again.

VOICE OF OLD MAN'S WIFE: Jean, don't stand gossiping, Jean!

BERENGER [*knocking*]: Jean!

OLD MAN [*to his wife*]: Just a moment. Oh dear, dear ... [*He closes the door and disappears.*]

JEAN [*still lying down, his back to the audience, in a hoarse voice*]: What is it?

BERENGER: I've dropped by to see you, Jean.

JEAN: Who is it?

BERENGER: It's me, Berenger. I hope I'm not disturbing you.

JEAN: Oh it's you, is it? Come in!

BERENGER [*trying to open the door*]: The door's locked.

JEAN: Just a moment. Oh dear, dear ... [JEAN *gets up in a pretty bad temper. He is wearing green pyjamas, his hair is tousled.*] Just a moment. [*He unlocks the door.*] Just a moment. [*He goes back to bed, gets under the blanket.*] Come in!

BERENGER [*coming in*]: Hello Jean!

JEAN [*in bed*]: What time is it? Aren't you at the office?

BERENGER: You're still in bed; you're not at the office, then? Sorry if I'm disturbing you.

JEAN [*still with his back turned*]: Funny, I didn't recognize your voice.

BERENGER: I didn't recognize yours either.

JEAN [*still with his back turned*]: Sit down!

BERENGER: Aren't you feeling well?

[JEAN *replies with a grunt.*]

You know, Jean, it was stupid of me to get so upset yesterday over a thing like that.

JEAN: A thing like what?

BERENGER: Yesterday ...

JEAN: When yesterday? Where yesterday?

BERENGER: Don't you remember? It was about that wretched rhinoceros.

JEAN: What rhinoceros?

BERENGER: The rhinoceros, or rather, the two wretched rhinoceroses we saw.

JEAN: Oh yes, I remember ... How do you know they were wretched?

BERENGER: Oh I just said that.

JEAN: Oh. Well let's not talk any more about it.

BERENGER: That's very nice of you.

JEAN: Then that's that.

BERENGER: But I would like to say how sorry I am for being so insistent ... and so obstinate ... and getting so angry ... in fact ... I acted stupidly.

JEAN: That's not surprising with you.

BERENGER: I'm very sorry.

JEAN: I don't feel very well. [*He coughs.*]

BERENGER: That's probably why you're in bed. [*With a change of tone*] You know, Jean, as it turned out, we were both right.

JEAN: What about?

BERENGER: About ... well, you know, the same thing. Sorry to bring it up again, but I'll only mention it briefly. I just wanted you to know that in our different ways we were both right. It's been proved now. There are some rhinoceroses in the town with two horns and some with one.

JEAN: That's what I told you! Well, that's just too bad.

BERENGER: Yes, too bad.

JEAN: Or maybe it's all to the good; it depends.

BERENGER [*continuing*]: In the final analysis it doesn't much matter which comes from where. The important thing, as I see it, is the fact that they're there at all, because ...

JEAN [*turning and sitting on his unmade bed, facing Berenger*]: I don't feel well, I don't feel well at all!

BERENGER: Oh I am sorry! What do you think it is?

JEAN: I don't know exactly, there's something wrong somewhere ...

BERENGER: Do you feel weak?

JEAN: Not at all. On the contrary, I feel full of beans.

BERENGER: I meant just a passing weakness. It happens to everybody.

JEAN: It never happens to me.

BERENGER: Perhaps you're too healthy then. Too much energy can be a bad thing. It unsettles the nervous system.

JEAN: My nervous system is in perfect order. [*His voice has become more and more hoarse.*] I'm sound in mind and limb. I come from a long line of ...

BERENGER: I know you do. Perhaps you've just caught a chill. Have you got a temperature?

JEAN: I don't know. Yes, probably I have a touch of fever. My head aches.

BERENGER: Just a slight migraine. Would you like me to leave you alone?

JEAN: No, stay. You don't worry me.

BERENGER: Your voice is hoarse, too.

JEAN: Hoarse?

BERENGER: A bit hoarse, yes. That's why I didn't recognize it.

JEAN: Why should I be hoarse? My voice hasn't changed; it's yours that's changed!

BERENGER: Mine?

JEAN: Why not?

BERENGER: It's possible. I hadn't noticed.

JEAN: I sometimes wonder if you're capable of noticing anything. [*Putting his hand to his forehead*] Actually it's my forehead that hurts. I must have given it a knock. [*His voice is even hoarser.*]

BERENGER: When did you do that?

JEAN: I don't know. I don't remember it happening.

BERENGER: But it must have hurt you.

JEAN: I must have done it while I was asleep.

BERENGER: The shock would have wakened you up. You must have just dreamed you knocked yourself.

JEAN: I never dream ...

BERENGER [*continuing*]: Your headache must have come on while you were asleep. You've forgotten you dreamed, or rather you only remember subconsciously.

JEAN: Subconsciously, me? I'm master of my own thoughts, my mind doesn't wander. I think straight, I always think straight.

BERENGER: I know that. I haven't made myself clear.

JEAN: Then make yourself clearer. And you needn't bother to make any of your unpleasant observations to me.

BERENGER: One often has the impression that one has knocked oneself when one has a headache. [*Coming closer to Jean*] If you'd really knocked yourself, you'd have a bump. [*Looking at Jean*] Oh, you've got one, you do have a bump, in fact.

JEAN: A bump?

BERENGER: Just a tiny one.

JEAN: Where?

BERENGER [*pointing to Jean's forehead*]: There, it starts just above your nose.

JEAN: I've no bump. We've never had bumps in my family.

BERENGER: Have you got a mirror?

JEAN: That's the limit! [*Touching his forehead*] I can feel something. I'm going to have a look, in the bathroom. [*He gets up abruptly and goes to the bathroom.* BERENGER *watches him as he goes. Then, from the bathroom*] It's true, I have got a bump. [*He comes back; his skin has become greener.*] So you see I did knock myself.

BERENGER: You don't look well, your skin is quite green.

JEAN: You seem to delight in saying disagreeable things to me. Have you taken a look at yourself lately?

BERENGER: Forgive me. I didn't mean to upset you.

JEAN [*very hoarse*]: That's hard to believe.

BERENGER: Your breathing's very heavy. Does your throat hurt?

[JEAN *goes and sits on his bed again.*]

If your throat hurts, perhaps it's a touch of quinsy.

JEAN: Why should I have a touch of quinsy?

BERENGER: It's nothing to be ashamed of – I sometimes get it. Let me feel your pulse. [*He rises and takes Jean's pulse.*]

JEAN [*in an even hoarser voice*]: Oh, it'll pass.

BERENGER: Your pulse is normal. You needn't get alarmed.

JEAN: I'm not alarmed in the slightest – why should I be?

BERENGER: You're right. A few days' rest will put you right.

JEAN: I've no time to rest. I must go and buy some food.

BERENGER: There's not much the matter with you, if you're hungry. But even so, you ought to take a few days' rest. It's wise to take care. Has the doctor been to see you?

JEAN: I don't need a doctor.

BERENGER: Oh, but you ought to get the doctor.

JEAN: You're not going to get the doctor because I don't want the doctor. I can look after myself.

BERENGER: You shouldn't reject medical advice.

JEAN: Doctors invent illnesses that don't exist.

BERENGER: They do it in good faith – just for the pleasure of looking after people.

JEAN: They invent illnesses, they invent them, I tell you.

BERENGER: Perhaps they do – but after they invent them they cure them.

JEAN: I only have confidence in veterinary surgeons. There!

BERENGER [who has released Jean's wrist, now takes it up again]: Your veins look swollen. They're jutting out.

JEAN: It's a sign of virility.

BERENGER: Of course it's a sign of health and strength. But ... [He examines Jean's forearm more closely, until Jean violently withdraws it.]

JEAN: What do you think you're doing – scrutinizing me as if I was some strange animal?

BERENGER: It's your skin ...

JEAN: What's my skin got to do with you? I don't go on about your skin, do I?

BERENGER: It's just that ... it seems to be changing colour all the time. It's going green. [He tries to take Jean's hand.] It's hardening as well.

JEAN [withdrawing his hand again]: Stop mauling me about! What's the matter with you? You're getting on my nerves.

BERENGER [*to himself*]: Perhaps it's more serious than I thought. [*To Jean*] We must get the doctor. [*He goes to the telephone.*]

JEAN: Leave that thing alone. [*He darts over to Berenger and pushes him.* BERENGER *staggers.*] You mind your own business.

BERENGER: All right. It was for your own good.

JEAN [*coughing and breathing noisily*]: I know better than you what's good for me.

BERENGER: You're breathing very hard.

JEAN: One breathes as best one can. You don't like the way I breathe, and I don't like the way you breathe. Your breathing's too feeble, you can't even hear it; it's as if you were going to drop dead any moment.

BERENGER: I know I'm not as strong as you.

JEAN: I don't keep trying to get you to the doctor, do I? Leave people to do as they please.

BERENGER: Don't get angry with me. You know very well I'm your friend.

JEAN: There's no such thing as friendship. I don't believe in your friendship.

BERENGER: That's a very hurtful thing to say.

JEAN: There's nothing for you to get hurt about.

BERENGER: My dear Jean ...

JEAN: I'm not your dear Jean.

BERENGER: You're certainly in a very misanthropic mood today.

JEAN: Yes, I am misanthropic, very misanthropic indeed. I like being misanthropic.

BERENGER: You're probably still angry with me over our silly quarrel yesterday. I admit it was my fault. That's why I came to say I was sorry ...

JEAN: What quarrel are you talking about?

BERENGER: I told you just now. You know, about the rhinoceros.

JEAN [*not listening to Berenger*]: It's not that I hate people. I'm just indifferent to them – or rather, they disgust me; and they'd better keep out of my way, or I'll run them down.

BERENGER: You know very well that I shall never stand in your way.

JEAN: I've got one aim in life. And I'm making straight for it.

BERENGER: I'm sure you're right. But I feel you're passing through a moral crisis.

[JEAN *has been pacing the room like a wild beast in a cage, from one wall to the other.* BERENGER *watches him, occasionally stepping aside to avoid him. Jean's voice has become more and more hoarse.*]

You mustn't excite yourself, it's bad for you.

JEAN: I felt uncomfortable in my clothes; now my pyjamas irritate me as well. [*He undoes his pyjama jacket and does it up again.*]

BERENGER: But whatever's the matter with your skin?

JEAN: Can't you leave my skin alone? I certainly wouldn't want to change it for yours.

BERENGER: It's gone like leather.

JEAN: That makes it more solid. It's weatherproof.

BERENGER: You're getting greener and greener.

JEAN: You've got colour mania today. You're seeing things, you've being drinking again.

BERENGER: I did yesterday, but not today.

JEAN: It's the result of all your past debauches.

BERENGER: I promised you to turn over a new leaf. I take notice when friends like you give me advice. And I never feel humiliated – on the contrary!

JEAN: I don't care what you feel. Brrr ...

BERENGER: What did you say?

JEAN: I didn't say anything. I just went Brrrr ... because I felt like it.

BERENGER [*looking fixedly at Jean*]: Do you know what's happened to Boeuf? He's turned into a rhinoceros.

JEAN: What happened to Boeuf?

BERENGER: He's turned into a rhinoceros.

JEAN [*fanning himself with the flaps of his jacket*]: Brrr ...

BERENGER: Come on now, stop joking.

JEAN: I can puff if I want to, can't I? I've every right ... I'm in my own house.

BERENGER: I didn't say you couldn't.

JEAN: And I shouldn't if I were you. I feel hot, I feel hot. Brrr ... Just a moment. I must cool myself down.

BERENGER [*whilst JEAN darts to the bathroom*]: He must have a fever.

[*JEAN is in the bathroom, one hears him puffing, and also the sound of a running tap.*]

JEAN [*off*]: Brrr ...

BERENGER: He's got the shivers. I'm jolly well going to phone the doctor. [*He goes to the telephone again then comes back quickly when he hears Jean's voice.*]

JEAN [*off*]: So old Boeuf turned into a rhinoceros, did he? Ah, ah, ah...! He was just having you on, he'd disguised himself. [*He pokes his head round the bathroom door. He is very green. The bump over his nose is slightly larger.*] He was just disguised.

BERENGER [*walking about the room, without seeing Jean*]: He looked very serious about it, I assure you.

JEAN: Oh well, that's his business.

BERENGER [*turning to Jean who disappears again into the bathroom*]: I'm sure he didn't do it on purpose. He didn't want to change.

JEAN [*off*]: How do you know?

BERENGER: Well, everything led one to suppose so.

JEAN: And what if he did do it on purpose? Eh? What if he did it on purpose?

77

BERENGER: I'd be very surprised. At any rate, Mrs Boeuf didn't seem to know about it ...

JEAN [*in a very hoarse voice*]: Ah, ah, ah! Fat old Mrs Boeuf. She's just a fool!

BERENGER: Well fool or no fool ...

JEAN [*he enters swiftly, takes off his jacket, and throws it on the bed.* BERENGER *discreetly averts his gaze.* JEAN, *whose back and chest are now green, goes back into the bathroom. As he walks in and out*] Boeuf never let his wife know what he was up to ...

BERENGER: You're wrong there, Jean – it was a very united family.

JEAN: Very united, was it? Are you sure? Hum, hum. Brr ...

BERENGER [*moving to the bathroom, where* JEAN *slams the door in his face*]: Very united. And the proof is that ...

JEAN [*from within*]: Boeuf led his own private life. He had a secret side to him deep down which he kept to himself.

BERENGER: I shouldn't make you talk, it seems to upset you.

JEAN: On the contrary, it relaxes me.

BERENGER: Even so, let me call the doctor, I beg you.

JEAN: I absolutely forbid it. I can't stand obstinate people.

[JEAN *comes back into the bedroom.* BERENGER *backs away a little scared, for* JEAN *is greener than ever and speaks only with difficulty. His voice is unrecognizable.*]

Well, whether he changes into a rhinoceros on purpose or against his will, he's probably all the better for it.

BERENGER: How can you say a thing like that? Surely you don't think ...

JEAN: You always see the black side of everything. It obviously gave him great pleasure to turn into a rhinoceros. There's nothing extraordinary in that.

BERENGER: There's nothing extraordinary in it, but I doubt if it gave him much pleasure.

JEAN: And why not, pray?

BERENGER: It's hard to say exactly why; it's just something you feel.

JEAN: I tell you it's not as bad as all that. After all, rhinoceros are living creatures the same as us; they've got as much right to life as we have!

BERENGER: As long as they don't destroy ours in the process. You must admit the difference in mentality.

JEAN [*pacing up and down the room, and in and out of the bathroom*]: Are you under the impression that our way of life is superior?

BERENGER: Well at any rate, we have our own moral standards which I consider incompatible with the standards of these animals.

JEAN: Moral standards! I'm sick of moral standards! We need to go beyond moral standards!

BERENGER: What would you put in their place?

JEAN [*still pacing*]: Nature!

BERENGER: Nature?

JEAN: Nature has its own laws. Morality's against Nature.

BERENGER: Are you suggesting we replace our moral laws by the law of the jungle?

JEAN: It would suit me, suit me fine.

BERENGER: You say that. But deep down, no one ...

JEAN [*interrupting him, pacing up and down*]: We've got to build our life on new foundations. We must get back to primeval integrity.

BERENGER: I don't agree with you at all.

JEAN [*breathing noisily*]: I can't breathe.

BERENGER: Just think a moment. You must admit that we have a philosophy that animals don't share, and an irreplaceable set of values, which it's taken centuries of human civilization to build up ...

JEAN [*in the bathroom*]: When we've demolished all that, we'll be better off!

79

BERENGER: I know you don't mean that seriously. You're joking! It's just a poetic fancy.

JEAN: Brrr. [*He almost trumpets.*]

BERENGER: I'd never realized you were a poet.

JEAN [*comes out of the bathroom*]: Brrr. [*He trumpets again.*]

BERENGER: That's not what you believe fundamentally – I know you too well. You know as well as I do that mankind ...

JEAN [*interrupting him*]: Don't talk to me about mankind!

BERENGER: I mean the human individual, humanism ...

JEAN: Humanism is all washed up! You're a ridiculous old sentimentalist. [*He goes into the bathroom.*]

BERENGER: But you must admit that the mind ...

JEAN [*from the bathroom*]: Just clichés! You're talking rubbish!

BERENGER: Rubbish!

JEAN [*from the bathroom in a very hoarse voice, difficult to understand*]: Utter rubbish!

BERENGER: I'm amazed to hear you say that, Jean, really! You must be out of your mind. You wouldn't like to be a rhinoceros yourself, now would you?

JEAN: Why not? I'm not a victim of prejudice like you.

BERENGER: Can you speak more clearly? I didn't catch what you said. You swallowed the words.

JEAN [*still in the bathroom*]: Then keep your ears open.

BERENGER: What?

JEAN: Keep your ears open. I said what's wrong with being a rhinoceros? I'm all for change.

BERENGER: It's not like you to say a thing like that ...

[BERENGER *stops short, for* JEAN'S *appearance is truly alarming. Jean has become, in fact, completely green. The bump on his forehead is practically a rhinoceros horn.*]

Oh! You really must be out of your mind!

[JEAN *dashes to his bed, throws the covers on the floor, talking in a fast and furious gabble, and making very weird sounds.*]

You mustn't get into such a state – calm down! I hardly recognize you any more.

JEAN [*hardly distinguishable*]: Hot ... far too hot! Demolish the lot, clothes itch, they itch! [*He drops his pyjama trousers.*]

BERENGER: What are you doing? You're not yourself! You're generally so modest!

JEAN: The swamps! The swamps!

BERENGER: Look at me! Can't you see me any longer? Can't you hear me?

JEAN: I can hear you perfectly well! I can see you perfectly well! [*He lunges towards Berenger, head down.* BERENGER *gets out of the way.*]

BERENGER: Watch out!

JEAN [*puffing noisily*]: Sorry! [*He darts at great speed into the bathroom.*]

BERENGER [*makes as if to escape by the door left, then comes back and goes into the bathroom after Jean, saying*]: I really can't leave him like that – after all he is a friend. [*From the bathroom*] I'm going to get the doctor! It's absolutely necessary, believe me!

JEAN [*from the bathroom*]: No!

BERENGER [*from the bathroom*]: Calm down, Jean, you're being ridiculous! Oh, your horn's getting longer and longer – you're a rhinoceros!

JEAN [*from the bathroom*]: I'll trample you, I'll trample you down!

[*A lot of noise comes from the bathroom, trumpetings, objects falling, the sound of a shattered mirror; then* BERENGER *reappears, very frightened; he closes the bathroom door with difficulty against the resistance that is being made from inside.*]

BERENGER [*pushing against the door*]: He's a rhinoceros, he's a rhinoceros!

[BERENGER *manages to close the door. As he does so, his coat is pierced by a rhinoceros horn. The door shakes under the animal's constant pressure and the din continues in the bath-room; trumpetings are heard, intercepted with indistinct phrases such as: 'I'm furious! The swine!' etc.* BERENGER *rushes to the door right.*]

I never would have thought it of him – never!

[*He opens the staircase door and goes and knocks at the landing door; he bangs repeatedly on it with his fist.*]

There's a rhinoceros in the building! Get the police!

OLD MAN [*poking his head out*]: What's the matter?

BERENGER: Get the police! There's a rhinoceros in the house!

VOICE OF OLD MAN'S WIFE: What are you up to, Jean? Why are you making all that noise?

OLD MAN [*to his wife*]: I don't know what he's talking about. He's seen a rhinoceros.

BERENGER: Yes, here in the house. Get the police!

OLD MAN: What do you think you're up to, disturbing people like that. What a way to behave! [*He shuts the door in his face.*]

BERENGER [*rushing to the stairs*]: Porter, porter, there's a rhinoceros in the house, get the police! Porter!

[*The upper part of the porter's lodge is seen to open; the head of a rhinoceros appears.*]

Another!

[BERENGER *rushes upstairs again. He wants to go back into Jean's room, hesitates, then makes for the door of the Old Man again. At this moment the door of the room opens to reveal two rhinoceros heads.*]

Oh, my God!

[BERENGER *goes back into Jean's room where the bathroom door is shaking. He goes to the window which is represented simply by the frame, facing the audience. He is exhausted, almost fainting; he murmurs.*]

My God! Oh my God!

[*He makes a gigantic effort, and manages to get astride the window (that is, towards the audience) but gets back again quickly, for at the same time, crossing the orchestra pit at great speed, move a large number of rhinoceros heads in line.* BERENGER *gets back with all speed, looks out of the window for a moment.*]

There's a whole herd of them in the street now! An army of rhinoceroses, surging up the avenue … ! [*He looks all around.*] Where can I get out? Where can I get out? If only they'd keep to the middle of the road! They're all over the pavement as well. Where can I get out? Where can I get out?

[*Distracted, he goes from door to door and to the window, whilst the bathroom door continues to shake and* JEAN *continues to trumpet and hurl incomprehensible insults. This continues for some moments; whenever* BERENGER, *in his disordered attempts to escape, reaches the door of the Old People's flat or the stairway, he is greeted by rhinoceros heads which trumpet and cause him to beat a hasty retreat. He goes to the window for the last time and looks out.*]

A whole herd of them! And they always said the rhinoceros was a solitary animal! That's not true, that's a conception they'll have to revise! They've smashed up all the public benches. [*He wrings his hands.*] What's to be done?

[*He goes once more to the various exits, but the spectacle of the rhinoceros halts him. When he gets back to the bathroom door it seems about to give way.* BERENGER *throws himself against the back wall, which yields; the street is visible in the background; he flees, shouting:*]

Rhinoceros! Rhinoceros!

[*Noises. The bathroom door is on the point of yielding.*]

CURTAIN

ACT THREE

The arrangement is roughly the same as in the previous scene.
It is Berenger's room, which bears a striking resemblance to that
of Jean's. Only certain details, one or two extra pieces of furniture,
reveal that it is a different room. Staircase to the left, and landing.
Door at the end of the landing. There is no porter's lodge. Up-stage
is a divan.
An armchair, and a little table with a telephone. Perhaps an extra
telephone, and a chair. Window up-stage, open. A window frame
in the foreground.

> [BERENGER *is lying on his divan, his back to the audience.*
> *Berenger is lying fully dressed. His head is bandaged. He seems*
> *to be having a bad dream, and writhes in his sleep.*]

BERENGER: No. [*Pause*] Watch out for the horns! [*Pause*]

> [*The noise of a considerable number of rhinoceroses is heard*
> *passing under the up-stage window.*]

No! [*He falls to the floor still fighting with what he has seen in*
his dream, and wakes up. He puts his hand to his head with an
apprehensive air, then moves to the mirror and lifts his bandage,
as the noises fade away. He heaves a sigh of relief when he sees
he has no bump. He hesitates, goes to the divan, lies down, and
instantly gets up again. He goes to the table where he takes up a
bottle of brandy and a glass, and is about to pour himself a drink.
Then after a short internal struggle he replaces the bottle and glass.]
Now, now, where's your will-power! [*He wants to go back*
to his divan, but the rhinoceroses are heard again under the up-
stage window. The noises stop; he goes to the little table, hesitates
a moment, then with a gesture of 'Oh what's it matter!' he pours
himself a glass of brandy which he downs at one go. He puts the

84

*bottle and glass back in place. He coughs. His cough seems to
worry him; he coughs again and listens hard to the sound. He
looks at himself again in the mirror, coughing, then opens the
window; the panting of the animals becomes louder; he coughs
again.]* No, it's not the same! *[He calms down, shuts the
window, feels his bandaged forehead, goes to his divan, and seems
to fall asleep.]*

   *[*DUDARD *is seen mounting the top stairs; he gets to the
   landing and knocks on Berenger's door.]*

BERENGER *[starting up]*: What is it?

DUDARD: I've dropped by to see you, Berenger.

BERENGER: Who is it?

DUDARD: It's me.

BERENGER: Who's me?

DUDARD: Me, Dudard.

BERENGER: Ah, it's you, come in!

DUDARD: I hope I'm not disturbing you. *[He tries to open the
door.]* The door's locked.

BERENGER: Just a moment. Oh dear, dear! *[He opens the
door.* DUDARD *enters.]*

DUDARD: Hello Berenger.

BERENGER: Hello Dudard, what time is it?

DUDARD: So, you're still barricaded in your room! Feeling
any better, old man?

BERENGER: Forgive me, I didn't recognize your voice. *[Goes
to open the window.]* Yes, yes, I think I'm a bit better.

DUDARD: My voice hasn't changed. I recognized yours easily
enough.

BERENGER: I'm sorry, I thought that ... you're right, your
voice is quite normal. Mine hasn't changed either, has it?

DUDARD: Why should it have changed?

BERENGER: I'm not a bit ... a bit hoarse, am I?

DUDARD: Not that I notice.

BERENGER: That's good. That's very reassuring.

DUDARD: Why, what's the matter with you?

BERENGER: I don't know – does one ever know? Voices can suddenly change – they do change, alas!

DUDARD: Have you caught cold, as well?

BERENGER: I hope not ... I sincerely hope not. But do sit down, Dudard, take a seat. Sit in the armchair.

DUDARD [sitting in the armchair]: Are you still feeling a bit off colour? Is your head still bad? [He points to Berenger's bandage.]

BERENGER: Oh yes, I've still got a headache. But there's no bump, I haven't knocked myself ... have I? [He lifts the bandage, shows his forehead to DUDARD.]

DUDARD: No, there's no bump as far as I can see.

BERENGER: I hope there never will be. Never.

DUDARD: If you don't knock yourself, why should there be?

BERENGER: If you really don't want to knock yourself, you don't.

DUDARD: Obviously. One just has to take care. But what's the matter with you? You're all nervous and agitated. It must be your migraine. You just stay quiet and you'll feel better.

BERENGER: Migraine! Don't talk to me about migraines! Don't talk about them!

DUDARD: It's understandable that you've got a migraine after all that emotion.

BERENGER: I can't seem to get over it!

DUDARD: Then it's not surprising you've got a headache.

BERENGER [darting to the mirror, lifting the bandage]: Nothing there ... You know, it can all start from something like that.

DUDARD: What can all start?

BERENGER: I'm frightened of becoming someone else.

DUDARD: Calm yourself, now, and sit down. Dashing up and down the room like that can only make you more nervous.

BERENGER: You're right, I must keep calm. [*He goes and sits down.*] I just can't get over it, you know.

DUDARD: About Jean you mean? – I know.

BERENGER: Yes, Jean, of course – and the others, too.

DUDARD: I realize it must have been a shock to you.

BERENGER: Well, that's not surprising, you must admit.

DUDARD: I suppose so, but you mustn't dramatize the situation; it's no reason for you to ...

BERENGER: I wonder how you'd have felt. Jean was my best friend. Then to watch him change before my eyes, and the way he got so furious!

DUDARD: I know. You felt let down; I understand. Try and not think about it.

BERENGER: How can I help thinking about it? He was such a warm-hearted person, always so human! Who'd have thought it of him! We'd known each other for ... for donkey's years. He was the last person I'd have expected to change like that. I felt more sure of him than of myself! And then to do that to me!

DUDARD: I'm sure he didn't do it specially to annoy you!

BERENGER: It seemed as if he did. If you'd seen the state he was in ... the expression on his face ...

DUDARD: It's just that you happened to be with him at the time. It would have been the same no matter who was there.

BERENGER: But after all our years together he might have controlled himself in front of me.

DUDARD: You think everything revolves round you, you think that everything that happens concerns you personally; you're not the centre of the universe, you know.

BERENGER: Perhaps you're right. I must try to readjust myself, but the phenomenon in itself is so disturbing. To tell the truth, it absolutely shatters me. What can be the explanation?

DUDARD: For the moment I haven't found a satisfactory explanation. I observe the facts, and I take them in. They exist, so they must have an explanation. A freak of Nature, perhaps, some bizarre caprice, an extravagant joke, a game – who knows?

BERENGER: Jean was very proud, of course. I'm not ambitious at all. I'm content to be what I am.

DUDARD: Perhaps he felt an urge for some fresh air, the country, the wide-open spaces ... perhaps he felt a need to relax. I'm not saying that's any excuse ...

BERENGER: I understand what you mean, at least I'm trying to. But you know – if someone accused me of being a bad sport, or hopelessly middle class, or completely out of touch with life, I'd still want to stay as I am.

DUDARD: We'll all stay as we are, don't worry. So why get upset over a few cases of rhinoceritis? Perhaps it's just another disease.

BERENGER: Exactly! And I'm frightened of catching it.

DUDARD: Oh stop thinking about it. Really, you attach too much importance to the whole business. Jean's case isn't symptomatic, he's not a typical case – you said yourself he was proud. In my opinion – if you'll excuse my saying this about your friend – he was far too excitable, a bit wild, an eccentric. You mustn't base your judgements on exceptions. It's the average case you must consider.

BERENGER: I'm beginning to see daylight. You see, you couldn't explain this phenomenon to me. And yet you just provided me with a plausible explanation. Yes, of course, he must have been in a critical condition to have got himself into that state. He must have been temporarily unbalanced. And yet he gave his reasons for it, he'd obviously given it a lot of thought, and weighed the pros and cons ... And what about Boeuf then, was he mad, too ... ? and wha about all the others ... ?

DUDARD: There's still the epidemic theory. It's like influenza. It's not the first time there's been an epidemic.

BERENGER: There's never been one like this. And what if it's come from the colonies?

DUDARD: In any case you can be sure that Boeuf and the others didn't do what they did – become what they became – just to annoy you. They wouldn't have gone to all that trouble.

BERENGER: That's true, that makes sense, it's a reassuring thought ... or on the other hand, perhaps that makes it worse? [*Rhinoceroses are heard, galloping under the up-stage window.*] There, you hear that? [*He darts to the window.*]

DUDARD: Oh, why can't you leave them alone!

[BERENGER *closes the window again.*]

They're not doing you any harm. Really, you're obsessed by them! It's not good for you. You're wearing yourself out. You've had one shock, why look for more? You just concentrate on getting back to normal.

BERENGER: I wonder if I really am immune?

DUDARD: In any case it's not fatal. Certain illnesses are good for you. I'm convinced this is something you can cure if you want to. They'll get over it, you'll see.

BERENGER: But it's bound to have certain after-effects! An organic upheaval like that can't help but leave ...

DUDARD: It's only temporary, don't you worry.

BERENGER: Are you absolutely certain!

DUDARD: I think so, yes, I suppose so.

BERENGER: But if one really doesn't want to, really doesn't want to catch this thing, which after all is a nervous disease – then you don't catch it, you simply don't catch it! Do you feel like a brandy? [*He goes to the table where the bottle stands.*]

DUDARD: Not for me, thank you, I never touch it. But don't mind me if you want some – you go ahead, don't worry about me. But watch out it doesn't make your headache worse.

BERENGER: Alcohol is good for epidemics. It immunizes you. It kills influenza microbes, for instance.

DUDARD: Perhaps it doesn't kill all microbes. They don't know about rhinoceritis yet.

BERENGER: Jean never touched alcohol. He just pretended to. Maybe that's why he ... perhaps that explains his attitude. [*He offers a full glass to Dudard.*] You're sure you won't?

DUDARD: No, no, never before lunch, thank you.

[BERENGER *empties his glass, continues to hold it, together with the bottle, in his hands; he coughs.*]

You see, you can't take it. It makes you cough.

BERENGER [*worried*]: Yes, it did make me cough. How did I cough?

DUDARD: Like everyone coughs when they drink something a bit strong.

BERENGER [*moving to put the glass and bottle back on the table*]: There wasn't anything odd about it, was there? It *was* a real human cough?

DUDARD: What are you getting at? It was an ordinary human cough. What other sort of cough could it have been?

BERENGER: I don't know ... Perhaps an animal's cough ... Do rhinoceroses cough?

DUDARD: Look, Berenger, you're being ridiculous, you invent difficulties for yourself, you ask yourself the weirdest questions ... I remember you said yourself that the best protection against the thing was will-power.

BERENGER: Yes, I did.

DUDARD: Well then, prove you've got some.

BERENGER: I have, I assure you ...

DUDARD: Prove it to yourself – now, don't drink any more brandy. You'll feel more sure of yourself then.

BERENGER: You deliberately misunderstand me. I told you

the only reason I take it is because it keeps the worst at bay; I'm doing it quite deliberately. When the epidemic's over, then I shall stop drinking. I'd already decided that before the whole business began. I'm just putting it off for the time being!

DUDARD: You're inventing excuses for yourself.

BERENGER: Do you think I am … ? In any case, that's got nothing to do with what's happening now.

DUDARD: How do we know?

BERENGER [*alarmed*]: Do you really think so? You think that's how the rot set in? I'm not an alcoholic. [*He goes to the mirror and examines himself.*] Do you think, by any chance … [*He touches his face, pats his bandaged forehead.*] Nothing's changed; it hasn't done any harm so it must have done good … or it's harmless at any rate.

DUDARD: I was only joking. I was just teasing you. You see the black side of everything – watch out, or you'll become a neurotic. When you've got over your shock completely and you can get out for a breath of fresh air, you'll feel better – you'll see! All these morbid ideas will vanish.

BERENGER: Go out? I suppose I'll have to. I'm dreading the moment. I'll be bound to meet some of them …

DUDARD: What if you do? You only have to keep out of their way. And there aren't as many as all that.

BERENGER: I see them all over the place. You'll probably say that's being morbid, too.

DUDARD: They don't attack you. If you leave them alone, they just ignore you. You can't say they're spiteful. They've even got a certain natural innocence, a sort of frankness. Besides I walked right along the avenue to get to you today. I got here safe and sound, didn't I? No trouble at all.

BERENGER: Just the sight of them upsets me. It's a nervous thing. I don't get angry – no, it doesn't pay to get angry, you never know where it'll lead to, I watch out for that.

But it does something to me, here! [*He points to his heart.*] I get a tight feeling inside.

DUDARD: I think you're right to a certain extent to have some reaction. But you go too far. You've no sense of humour, that's your trouble, none at all. You must learn to be more detached, and try and see the funny side of things.

BERENGER: I feel responsible for everything that happens. I feel involved, I just can't be indifferent.

DUDARD: Judge not lest ye be judged. If you start worrying about everything that happens you'd never be able to go on living.

BERENGER: If only it had happened somewhere else, in some other country, and we'd just read about it in the papers, one could discuss it quietly, examine the question from all points of view and come to an objective conclusion. We could organize debates with professors and writers and lawyers, and blue-stockings and artists and people. And the ordinary man in the street, as well – it would be very interesting and instructive. But when you're involved yourself, when you suddenly find yourself up against the brutal facts you can't help feeling directly concerned – the shock is too violent for you to stay cool and detached. I'm frankly surprised, I'm very very surprised. I can't get over it.

DUDARD: Well I'm surprised, too. Or rather I was. Now I'm starting to get used to it.

BERENGER: Your nervous system is better balanced than mine. You're lucky. But don't you agree it's all very unfortunate …

DUNARD [*interrupting him*]: I don't say it's a good thing. And don't get the idea that I'm on the rhinoceroses' side …

[*More sounds of rhinoceroses passing, this time under the down-stage window-frame.*]

BERENGER [*with a start*]: There they are, there they are again! Oh, it's no use, I just can't get used to them. Maybe it's wrong of me, but they obsess me so much in spite of my-self, I just can't sleep at night. I get insomnia. I doze a bit in the daytime out of sheer exhaustion.

DUDARD: Take some sleeping tablets.

BERENGER: That's not the answer. If I sleep, it's worse. I dream about them, I get nightmares.

DUDARD: That's what comes of taking things too seriously. You get a kick out of torturing yourself – admit it!

BERENGER: I'm no masochist, I assure you.

DUDARD: Then face the facts and get over it. This is the situation and there's nothing you can do about it.

BERENGER: That's fatalism.

DUDARD: It's common sense. When a thing like this happens there's bound to be a reason for it. That's what we must find out.

BERENGER [getting up]: Well, I don't want to accept the situation.

DUDARD: What else can you do? What are your plans?

BERENGER: I don't know for the moment. I must think it over. I shall write to the papers; I'll draw up manifestoes; I shall apply for an audience with the mayor – or his deputy, if the mayor's too busy.

DUDARD: You leave the authorities to act as they think best! I'm not sure if morally you have the right to butt in. In any case I still think it's not all that serious. I consider it's silly to get worked up because a few people decide to change their skins. They just didn't feel happy in the ones they had. They're free to do as they like.

BERENGER: We must attack the evil at the roots.

DUDARD: The evil! That's just a phrase! Who knows what is evil and what is good? It's just a question of personal pre-ferences. You're worried about your own skin – that's the truth of the matter. But you'll never become a rhinoceros, really you won't ... you haven't got the vocation!

BERENGER: There you are, you see! If our leaders and fellow citizens all think like you, they'll never take any action.

DUDARD: You wouldn't want to ask for help from abroad, surely? This is an internal affair, it only concerns our country.

BERENGER: I believe in international solidarity ...

DUDARD: You're a Don Quixote. Oh, I don't mean that nastily, don't be offended! I'm only saying it for your own good, because you really need to calm down.

BERENGER: You're right, I know – forgive me. I get too worked up. But I'll change, I will change. I'm sorry to keep you all this time listening to my ramblings. You must have work to do. Did you get my application for sick leave?

DUDARD: Don't worry about that. It's all in order. In any case, the office hasn't resumed work.

BERENGER: Haven't they repaired the staircase yet? What negligence! That's why everything goes so badly.

DUDARD: They're repairing it now. But it's slow work. It's not easy to find the workmen. They sign on and work for a couple of days, then don't turn up any more. You never see them again. Then you have to look for others.

BERENGER: And they talk about unemployment! At least I hope we're getting a stone staircase.

DUDARD: No, it's wood again, but new wood this time.

BERENGER: Oh! The way these organizations stick to the old routine. They chuck money down the drain but when it's needed for something really useful they pretend they can't afford it. I bet Mr Papillon's none too pleased. He was dead set on having a stone staircase. What's he say about it?

DUDARD: We haven't got a Chief any more. Mr Papillon's resigned.

BERENGER: It's not possible!

DUDARD: It's true, I assure you.

BERENGER: Well, I'm amazed ... Was it on account of the staircase?

DUDARD: I don't think so. Anyway that wasn't the reason he gave.

BERENGER: Why was it then? What got into him?

DUDARD: He's retiring to the country.

BERENGER: Retiring? He's not the age. He might still have become the Director.

DUDARD: He's given it all up! Said he needed a rest.

BERENGER: I bet the management's pretty upset to see him go; they'll have to replace him. All your diplomas should come in useful – you stand a good chance.

DUDARD: I suppose I might as well tell you ... it's really rather funny – the fact is, he turned into a rhinoceros.

[*Distant rhinoceros noises.*]

BERENGER: A rhinoceros ! ! ! ! Mr Papillon a rhinoceros! I can't believe it! I don't think it's funny at all! Why didn't you tell me before?

DUDARD: Well you know you've no sense of humour. I didn't want to tell you ... I didn't want to tell you because I knew very well you wouldn't see the funny side, and it would upset you. You know how impressionable you are!

BERENGER [*raising his arms to heaven*]: Oh that's awful ... Mr Papillon! And he had such a good job.

DUDARD: That proves his metamorphosis was sincere.

BERENGER: He couldn't have done it on purpose. I'm certain it must have been involuntary.

DUDARD: How can we tell? It's hard to know the real reasons for people's decisions.

BERENGER: He must have made a mistake. He'd got some hidden complexes. He should have been psychoanalysed.

DUDARD: Even if it's a case of dissociation it's still very revealing. It was his way of sublimating himself.

BERENGER: He let himself be talked into it, I feel sure.

DUDARD: That could happen to anybody!

BERENGER [*alarmed*]: To anybody? Oh no, not to you it couldn't – could it? And not to me!

DUDARD: We must hope not.

BERENGER: Because we don't want to ... that's so, isn't it? Tell me, that *is* so, isn't it?

DUDARD: Yes, yes, of course ...

BERENGER [*a little calmer*]: I still would have thought Mr Papillon would have had the strength to resist. I thought he had a bit more character! Particularly as I fail to see where his interest lay – what possible material or moral interest ...

DUDARD: It was obviously a disinterested gesture on his part.

BERENGER: Obviously. There were extenuating circumstances ... or were they aggravating? Aggravating, I should think, because if he did it from choice ... You know I feel sure that Botard must have taken a very poor view of it – what did he think of his Chief's behaviour?

DUDARD: Oh poor old Botard was quite indignant, absolutely outraged. I've rarely seen anyone so incensed.

BERENGER: Well for once I'm on his side. He's a good man after all. A man of sound common sense. And to think I misjudged him.

DUDARD: He misjudged you, too.

BERENGER: That proves how objective I'm being now. Besides, you had a pretty bad opinion of him yourself.

DUDARD: I wouldn't say I had a bad opinion. I admit I didn't often agree with him. I never liked his scepticism, the way he was always so incredulous and suspicious. Even in this instance I didn't approve of him entirely.

BERENGER: This time for the opposite reasons.

DUDARD: No, not exactly – my own reasoning and my judgement are a bit more complex than you seem to think. It was because there was nothing precise or objective about the way Botard argued. I don't approve of the rhinoceroses myself, as you know – not at all, don't go thinking that! But Botard's attitude was too passionate, as usual, and therefore over-simplified. His stand seems to me entirely dictated by hatred of his superiors. That's where he gets his inferiority complex and his resentment. What's more he talks in clichés, and commonplace arguments leave me cold.

BERENGER: Well forgive me, but this time I'm in complete agreement with Botard. He's somebody worthwhile.

DUDARD: I don't deny it, but that doesn't mean anything.

BERENGER: He's a very worthwhile person – and they're not easy to find these days. He's down-to-earth, with four feet planted firmly on the ground – I mean, both feet. I'm in complete agreement with him, and I'm proud of it. I shall congratulate him when I see him. I deplore Mr Papillon's action; it was his duty not to succumb.

DUDARD: How intolerant you are! Maybe Papillon felt the need for a bit of relaxation after all these years of office life.

BERENGER [ironically]: And you're too tolerant, far too broadminded!

DUDARD: My dear Berenger, one must always make an effort to understand. And in order to understand a phenomenon and its effects you need to work back to the initial causes, by honest intellectual effort. We must try to do this because, after all, we are thinking beings. I haven't yet succeeded, as I told you, and I don't know if I shall succeed. But in any case one has to start out favourably disposed – or at least, impartial; one has to keep an open mind – that's essential to a scientific mentality. Everything is logical. To understand is to justify.

BERENGER: You'll be siding with the rhinoceroses before long.

DUDARD: No, no, not at all. I wouldn't go that far. I'm simply trying to look the facts unemotionally in the face. I'm trying to be realistic. I also contend that there is no real evil in what

occurs naturally. I don't believe in seeing evil in everything.
I leave that to the inquisitors.

BERENGER: And you consider all this natural?

DUDARD: What could be more natural than a rhinoceros?

BERENGER: Yes, but for a man to turn into a rhinoceros is
abnormal beyond question.

DUDARD: Well, of course, that's a matter of opinion ...

BERENGER: It is beyond question, absolutely beyond question!

DUDARD: You seem very sure of yourself. Who can say
where the normal stops and the abnormal begins? Can you
personally define these conceptions of normality and ab-
normality? Nobody has solved this problem yet, either
medically or philosophically. You ought to know that.

BERENGER: The problem may not be resolved philosophically
– but in practice it's simple. They may prove there's no such
thing as movement ... and then you start walking ... [*He starts
walking up and down the room.*] ... and you go on walking,
and you say to yourself, like Galileo, '*E pur si muove*' ...

DUDARD: You're getting things all mixed up! Don't con-
fuse the issue. In Galileo's case it was the opposite: theoretic
and scientific thought proving itself superior to mass
opinion and dogmatism.

BERENGER [*quite lost*]: What does all that mean? Mass
opinion, dogmatism – they're just words! I may be mixing
everything up in my head but you're losing yours. You
don't know what's normal and what isn't any more. I
couldn't care less about Galileo ... I don't give a damn about
Galileo.

DUDARD: You brought him up in the first place and raised
the whole question, saying that practice always had the last
word. Maybe it does, but only when it proceeds from
theory! The history of thought and science proves that.

BERENGER [*more and more furious*]: It doesn't prove anything
of the sort! It's all gibberish, utter lunacy!

DUDARD: There again we need to define exactly what we mean by lunacy ...

BERENGER: Lunacy is lunacy and that's all there is to it! Everybody knows what lunacy is. And what about the rhinoceroses – are they practice or are they theory?

DUDARD: Both!

BERENGER: How do you mean – both?

DUDARD: Both the one and the other, or one or the other. It's a debatable point!

BERENGER: Well in that case ... I refuse to think about it!

DUDARD: You're getting all het up. Our opinions may not exactly coincide but we can still discuss the matter peaceably. These things should be discussed.

BERENGER [distracted]: You think I'm getting all het up, do you? I might be Jean. Oh no, no, I don't want to become like him. I mustn't be like him. [He calms down.] I'm not very well up in philosophy. I've never studied; you've got all sorts of diplomas. That's why you're so at ease in discussion, whereas I never know what to answer – I'm so clumsy. [Louder rhinoceros noises passing first under the up-stage window and then the down-stage.] But I do feel you're in the wrong ... I feel it instinctively – no, that's not what I mean, it's the rhinoceros which has instinct – I feel it intuitively, yes, that's the word, intuitively.

DUDARD: What do you understand by 'intuitive'?

BERENGER: Intuitively means ... well, just like that! I feel it, just like that. I think your excessive tolerance, and your generous indulgence ... believe me, they're really only weakness ... just blind spots ...

DUDARD: You're innocent enough to think that.

BERENGER: You'll always be able to dance rings round me. But, you know what? I'm going to try and get hold of the Logician ...

DUDARD: What logician?

BERENGER: The Logician, the philosopher, a logician, you know ... you know better than I do what a logician is. A logician I met, who explained to me ...

DUDARD: What did he explain to you?

BERENGER: He explained that the Asiatic rhinoceroses were African and the African ones Asiatic.

DUDARD: I don't follow you.

BERENGER: No ... no ... he proved the contrary – that the African ones were Asiatic and the Asiatic ones ... I know what I mean. That's not what I wanted to say. But you'll get on very well with him. He's your sort of person, a very good man, a very subtle mind, brilliant.

[*Increasing noises from the rhinoceroses. The words of the two men are drowned by the animals passing under the windows; for a few moments the lips of* DUDARD *and* BERENGER *are seen to move without any words being heard.*]

There they go again! Will they never stop! [*He runs to the up-stage window.*] Stop it! Stop it! You devils!

[*The rhinoceroses move away.* BERENGER *shakes his fist after them.*]

DUDARD [*seated*]: I'd be happy to meet your Logician. If he can enlighten me on these obscure and delicate points, I'd be only too delighted.

BERENGER [*as he runs to the down-stage window*]: Yes, I'll bring him along, he'll talk to you. He's a very distinguished person, you'll see. [*To the rhinoceroses, from the window*] You devils! [*Shakes his fist as before.*]

DUDARD: Let them alone. And be more polite. You shouldn't talk to people like that ...

BERENGER [*still at the window*]: There they go again!

[*A boater pierced by a rhinoceros horn emerges from the orchestra pit under the window and passes swiftly from left to right.*]

There's a boater impaled on a rhinoceros horn. Oh, it's the

Logician's hat! It's the Logician's! That's the bloody limit!
The Logician's turned into a rhinoceros!

DUDARD: That's no reason to be coarse!

BERENGER: Dear Lord, who can you turn to – who? I ask
you! The Logician a rhinoceros!

DUDARD [*going to the window*]: Where is he?

BERENGER [*pointing*]: There, that one there, you see!

DUDARD: He's the only rhinoceros in a boater! That makes
you think. You're sure it's your Logician?

BERENGER: The Logician ... a rhinoceros! ! !

DUDARD: He's still retained a vestige of his old individuality.

BERENGER [*shakes his fist again at the straw-hatted rhinoceros,
which has disappeared*]: I'll never join up with you! Not
me!

DUDARD: If he was a genuine thinker, as you say, he couldn't
have got carried away. He must have weighed all the pros
and cons before deciding.

BERENGER [*still shouting after the ex-Logician and the other
rhinoceroses who have moved away*]: I'll never join up with
you!

DUDARD [*settling into the armchair*]: Yes, that certainly makes
you think!

[BERENGER *closes the down-stage window; goes to the up-
stage window where other rhinoceroses are passing, presumably
making a tour of the house. He opens the window and shouts.*]

BERENGER: No, I'll never join up with you!

DUDARD [*aside, in his armchair*]: They're going round and
round the house. They're playing! Just big babies!

[DAISY *has been seen mounting the top stairs. She knocks on
Berenger's door. She is carrying a basket.*]

There's somebody at the door, Berenger!

[*He takes Berenger, who is still at the window, by the sleeve.*]

BERENGER [*shouting after the rhinoceroses*]: It's a disgrace,
masquerading like this, a disgrace!

DUDARD: There's someone knocking, Berenger, can't you hear?

BERENGER: Open, then, if you want to! [*He continues to watch the rhinoceroses whose noise is fading away.*]

[DUDARD *goes to open the door.*]

DAISY [*coming in*]: Morning, Mr Dudard.

DUDARD: Oh, it's you, Miss Daisy.

DAISY: Is Berenger here, is he any better?

DUDARD: How nice to see you, my dear. Do you often visit Berenger?

DAISY: Where is he?

DUDARD [*pointing*]: There.

DAISY: He's all on his own, poor thing. And he's not very well at the moment, somebody has to give him a hand.

DUDARD: You're a good friend, Miss Daisy.

DAISY: That's just what I am, a good friend.

DUDARD: You've got a warm heart.

DAISY: I'm a good friend, that's all.

BERENGER [*turning, leaving the window open*]: Oh Miss Daisy! How kind of you to come, how very kind!

DUDARD: It certainly is.

BERENGER: Did you know, Miss Daisy, that the Logician is a rhinoceros?

DAISY: Yes, I did. I caught sight of him in the street as I arrived. He was running very fast for someone his age! Are you feeling any better, Mr Berenger?

BERENGER: My head's still bad! Still got a headache! Isn't it frightful? What do you think about it?

DAISY: I think you ought to be resting ... you should take things quietly for a few more days.

DUDARD [*to Berenger and Daisy*]: I hope I'm not disturbing you!

BERENGER [*to Daisy*]: I meant about the Logician ...

DAISY [*to Dudard*]: Why should you be? [*To Berenger*] Oh, about the Logician? I don't think anything at all!

DUDARD [*to Daisy*]: I thought I might be in the way!

DAISY [*to Berenger*]: What do you expect me to think? [*To both*] I've got some news for you: Botard's a rhinoceros!

DUDARD: Well, well!

BERENGER: I don't believe it. He was against it. You must be mistaken. He protested. Dudard has just been telling me. Isn't that so, Dudard?

DUDARD: That is so.

DAISY: I know he was against it. But it didn't stop him turning, twenty-four hours after Mr Papillon.

DUDARD: Well, he must have changed his mind! Everybody has the right to do that.

BERENGER: Then obviously anything can happen!

DUDARD [*to Berenger*]: He was a very good man according to you just now.

BERENGER [*to Daisy*]: I just can't believe you. They must have lied to you.

DAISY: I saw him do it.

BERENGER: Then he must have been lying; he was just pretending.

DAISY: He seemed very sincere; sincerity itself.

BERENGER: Did he give any reasons?

DAISY: What he said was: we must move with the times! Those were his last human words.

DUDARD [*to Daisy*]: I was almost certain I'd meet you here, Miss Daisy.

BERENGER: ... Move with the times! What a mentality! [*He makes a wide gesture.*]

DUDARD [*to Daisy*]: Impossible to find you anywhere else, since the office closed.

BERENGER [*continuing, aside*]: What childishness! [*He repeats the same gesture.*]

DAISY [*to Dudard*]: If you wanted to see me, you only had to telephone.

DUDARD [*to Daisy*]: Oh you know me, Miss Daisy, I'm discretion itself.

BERENGER: But now I come to think it over, Botard's behaviour doesn't surprise me. His firmness was only a pose. Which doesn't stop him from being a good man, of course. Good men make good rhinoceroses, unfortunately. It's because they are so good that they get taken in.

DAISY: Do you mind if I put this basket on the table? [*She does so.*]

BERENGER: But he was a good man with a lot of resentment ...

DUDARD [*to Daisy, and hastening to help her with the basket*]: Excuse me, excuse us both, we should have given you a hand before.

BERENGER [*continues*]: ... He was riddled with hatred for his superiors, and he'd got an inferiority complex. ...

DUDARD [*to Berenger*]: Your argument doesn't hold water, because the example he followed was the Chief's, the very instrument of the people who exploited him, as he used to say. No, it seems to me that with him it was a case of community spirit triumphing over his anarchic impulses.

BERENGER: It's the rhinoceroses which are anarchic, because they're in the minority.

DUDARD: They are, it's true – for the moment.

DAISY: They're a pretty big minority, and getting bigger all the time. My cousin's a rhinoceros now, and his wife. Not to mention leading personalities like the Cardinal of Retz ...

DUDARD: A prelate!

DAISY: Mazarin.

DUDARD: This is going to spread to other countries, you'll see.

BERENGER: And to think it all started with us!

DAISY: ... and some of the aristocracy. The Duke of St Simon.

BERENGER [*with uplifted arms*]: All our great names!

DAISY: And others, too. Lots of others. Maybe a quarter of the whole town.

BERENGER: We're still in the majority. We must take advantage of that. We must do something before we're inundated.

DUDARD: They're very potent, very.

DAISY: Well for the moment, let's eat. I've brought some food.

BERENGER: You're very kind, Miss Daisy.

DUDARD [*aside*]: Very kind indeed.

BERENGER: I don't know how to thank you.

DAISY [*to Dudard*]: Would you care to stay with us?

DUDARD: I don't want to be a nuisance.

DAISY: Whatever do you mean, Mr Dudard? You know very well we'd love you to stay.

DUDARD: Well, you know, I'd hate to be in the way ...

BERENGER: Of course, stay, Dudard. It's always a pleasure to talk to you.

DUDARD: As a matter of fact I'm in a bit of a hurry. I have an appointment.

BERENGER: Just now you said you'd got nothing to do.

DAISY [*unpacking her basket*]: You know, I had a lot of trouble finding food. The shops have been plundered; they just devour everything. And a lot of the shops are closed. It's written up outside: 'Closed on account of transformation.'

BERENGER: They should all be rounded up in a big enclosure, and kept under strict supervision.

DUDARD: That's easier said than done. The animals' protection league would be the first to object.

DAISY: And besides everyone has a close relative or a friend among them, and that would make it even more difficult.

BERENGER: So everybody's mixed up in it!

DUDARD: Everybody's in the same boat!

BERENGER: But how can people be rhinoceroses? It doesn't bear thinking about! [*To Daisy*] Shall I help you lay the table?

DAISY: No, don't bother. I know where the plates are. [*She goes to a cupboard and takes out the plates.*]

DUDARD [*aside*]: She's obviously very familiar with the place ...

DAISY [*to Dudard*]: I'm laying for three – all right? You are staying with us?

BERENGER [*to Dudard*]: Yes, of course you're staying.

DAISY [*to Berenger*]: You get used to it, you know. Nobody seems surprised any more to see herds of rhinoceros galloping through the streets. They just stand aside, and then carry on as if nothing had happened.

DUDARD: It's the wisest course to take.

BERENGER: Well I can't get used to it.

DUDARD [*reflectively*]: I wonder if one oughtn't to give it a try?

DAISY: Well right now, let's have lunch.

BERENGER: I don't see how a legal man like yourself can ...

[*A great noise of rhinoceroses travelling very fast is heard outside. Trumpets and drums are also heard.*]

What's going on?

[*They rush to the down-stage window.*]

What is it?

[*The sound of a wall crumbling is heard. Dust covers part of the stage, enveloping if possible the characters. They are heard speaking through it.*]

BERENGER: You can't see a thing! What's happening?

DUDARD: You can't see, but you can hear all right.

BERENGER: That's no good!

DAISY: The plates will all be covered in dust.

BERENGER: How unhygienic!

DAISY: Let's hurry up and eat. We won't pay any attention to them.

[*The dust disperses.*]

BERENGER [*pointing into the auditorium*]: They've demolished the walls of the Fire Station.

DUDARD: That's true, they've demolished them!

DAISY [*who after moving from the window to near the table holding the plate which she is endeavouring to clean, rushes to join the other two*]: They're coming out.

BERENGER: All the firemen, a whole regiment of rhinoceros, led by drums.

DAISY: They're pouring up the streets!

BERENGER: It's gone too far, much too far!

DAISY: More rhinoceroses are streaming out of the court-yard.

BERENGER: And out of the houses ...

DUDARD: And the windows as well!

DAISY: They're joining up with the others.

[*A man comes out of the landing door left and dashes downstairs at top speed; then another with a large horn on his nose; then a woman wearing an entire rhinoceros head.*]

DUDARD: There aren't enough of us left any more.

BERENGER: How many with one horn, and how many with two?

DUDARD: The statisticians are bound to be compiling statistics now. There'll be plenty of erudite controversy you can be sure!

BERENGER: They can only calculate approximately. It's all happening so fast. It leaves them no time. No time to calculate.

DAISY: The best thing is to let the statisticians get on with it. Come and eat, my dear. That'll calm you down. You'll feel better afterwards. [*To Dudard*] And you, too.

[*They move away from the window.* DAISY *takes Berenger's*

arm; he allows himself to be led docilely. DUDARD *suddenly halts.*]

DUDARD: I don't feel very hungry – or rather, to be frank, I don't like tinned food very much. I feel like eating outside on the grass.

BERENGER: You mustn't do that. Think of the risk!

DUDARD: But really I don't want to put you to the trouble.

BERENGER: But we've already told you ...

DUDARD [*interrupting Berenger*]: I really mean it.

DAISY [*to Dudard*]: Of course if you really don't want to stay, we can't force you ...

DUDARD: I didn't mean to offend you.

BERENGER [*to Daisy*]: Don't let him go, he mustn't go.

DAISY: I'd like him to stay ... but people must do as they please.

BERENGER [*to Dudard*]: Man is superior to the rhinoceros.

DUDARD: I didn't say he wasn't. But I'm not with you absolutely either. I don't know; only experience can tell.

BERENGER [*to Dudard*]: You're weakening too, Dudard. It's just a passing phase which you'll regret.

DAISY: If it's just a passing phase then there's no great danger.

DUDARD: I feel certain scruples! I feel it's my duty to stick by my employers and my friends, through thick and thin.

BERENGER: It's not as if you were married to them.

DUDARD: I've renounced marriage. I prefer the great universal family to the little domestic one.

DAISY [*softly*]: We shall miss you a lot, Dudard, but we can't do anything about it.

DUDARD: It's my duty to stick by them; I have to do my duty.

BERENGER: No you're wrong, your duty is to ... you don't see where your real duty lies ... your duty is to oppose them, with a firm, clear mind.

DUDARD: I shall keep my mind clear. [*He starts to move round the stage in circles.*] As clear as ever it was. But if you're going to criticize, it's better to do so from the inside. I'm not going to abandon them. I won't abandon them.

DAISY: He's very good-hearted.

BERENGER: He's too good-hearted. [*To Dudard, then dashing to the door*] You're too good-hearted, you're mistaken. [*To Daisy*] Don't let him go. He's making a mistake. He's human.

DAISY: What can I do?

[DUDARD *opens the door and runs off; he goes down the stairs at top speed followed by* BERENGER *who shouts after him from the landing.*]

BERENGER: Come back, Dudard! We're fond of you, don't go! It's too late! [*He comes back.*] Too late!

DAISY: We couldn't do anything. [*She closes the door behind* BERENGER, *who darts to the down-stage window.*]

BERENGER: He's joined up with them. Where is he now?

DAISY [*moving to the window*]: With them.

BERENGER: Which one is he?

DAISY: You can't tell. You can't recognize him any more.

BERENGER: They all look alike, all alike. [*To Daisy*] He *did* hesitate. You should have held him back by force.

DAISY: I didn't dare to.

BERENGER: You should have been firmer with him, you should have insisted; he was in love with you, wasn't he?

DAISY: He never made any official declaration.

BERENGER: Everybody knew he was. He's done this out of thwarted love. He was a shy man. He wanted to make a big gesture to impress you. Don't you feel like going after him?

DAISY: Not at all. Or I wouldn't be here!

BERENGER [*looking out of the window*]: You can see nothing but them in the street. [*He darts to the up-stage window.*] Nothing but them! You were wrong, Daisy. [*He looks through the down-stage window again.*] Not a single human being as far as the eye can see. They're all over the street. Half with one horn and half with two, and that's the only distinction!

[*Powerful noises of moving rhinoceroses are heard, but somehow it is a musical sound. On the up-stage wall stylized heads appear and disappear; they become more and more numerous from now on until the end of the play. Towards the end they stay fixed for longer and longer, until eventually they fill the entire back wall, remaining static. The heads, in spite of their monstrous appearance, seem to become more and more beautiful.*]

You don't feel let down, do you, Daisy? There's nothing you regret?

DAISY: No, no.

BERENGER: I want so much to be a comfort to you. I love you, Daisy; don't ever leave me.

DAISY: Shut the window, darling. They're making such a noise. And the dust is rising even up to here. Everything will get filthy.

BERENGER: Yes, you're right. [*He closes the down-stage window and* DAISY *closes the up-stage one. They meet centre-stage.*] I'm not afraid of anything as long as we're together. I don't care what happens. You know, Daisy, I thought I'd never be able to fall in love again. [*He takes her hands, strokes her arms.*]

DAISY: Well you see, everything is possible.

BERENGER: I want so much to make you happy. Do you think you can be happy with me?

DAISY: Why not? If you're happy, then I'll be happy too. You say nothing scares you, but you're really frightened of everything. What can possibly happen to us?

BERENGER [*stammering*]: My love, my dear love ... let me kiss your lips. I never dreamed I could still feel such tremendous emotion!

DAISY: You must be more calm and more sure of yourself, now.

BERENGER: I am; let me kiss you.

DAISY: I'm very tired, dear. Stay quiet and rest yourself. Sit in the armchair.

[BERENGER, *led by* DAISY, *sits in the armchair*.]

BERENGER: There was no point in Dudard quarrelling with Botard, as things turned out.

DAISY: Don't think about Dudard any more. I'm here with you. We've no right to interfere in other people's lives.

BERENGER: But you're interfering in mine. You know how to be firm with me.

DAISY: That's not the same thing; I never loved Dudard.

BERENGER: I see what you mean. If he'd stayed he'd always have been an obstacle between us. Ah, happiness is such an egotistical thing!

DAISY: You have to fight for happiness, don't you agree?

BERENGER: I adore you, Daisy; I admire you as well.

DAISY: Maybe you won't say that when you get to know me better.

BERENGER: The more I know you the better you seem; and you're so beautiful, so very beautiful. [*More rhinoceroses are heard passing.*] Particularly compared with them ... [*He points to the window.*] You probably think that's no compliment, but they make you seem more beautiful than ever ...

DAISY: Have you been good today? You haven't had any brandy?

BERENGER: Oh yes, I've been good.

DAISY: Is that the truth?

BERENGER: Yes, it's the truth I assure you.

DAISY: Can I believe you, I wonder?

BERENGER [*a little flustered*]: Oh yes, you must believe me.

DAISY: Well all right then, you can have a little glass. It'll buck you up.

[BERENGER *is about to leap up.*]

You stay where you are, dear. Where's the bottle?

BERENGER [*pointing to it*]: There, on the little table.

DAISY [*going to the table and getting the bottle and glass*]: You've hidden it well away.

BERENGER: It's out of the way of temptation.

DAISY [*pours a small glass*]: You've been a good boy. You're making progress.

BERENGER: I'll make a lot more now I'm with you.

DAISY [*handing him the glass*]: Here you are. That's your reward.

BERENGER [*downing it at one go*]: Thank you. [*He holds up his empty glass to Daisy.*]

DAISY: Oh no, dear. That's enough for this morning. [*She takes his glass, puts it back on the table with the bottle.*] I don't want it to make you ill. [*She comes back to him.*] How's your head feel now?

BERENGER: Much better, darling.

DAISY: Then we'll take off the bandage. It doesn't suit you at all.

BERENGER: Oh no, don't touch it.

DAISY: Nonsense, we'll take it off now.

BERENGER: I'm frightened there might be something underneath.

DAISY [*removing the bandage in spite of his protests*]: Always frightened, aren't you, always imagining the worst! There's nothing there, you see. Your forehead's as smooth as a baby's.

BERENGER [*feeling his brow*]: You're right; you're getting rid of my complexes. [DAISY *kisses him on the brow.*] What should I do without you?

DAISY: I'll never leave you alone again.

BERENGER: I won't have any more fears now I'm with you.

DAISY: I'll keep them all at bay.

BERENGER: We'll read books together. I'll become clever.

DAISY: And when there aren't so many people about we'll go for long walks.

BERENGER: Yes, along the Seine, and in the Luxembourg Gardens ...

DAISY: And to the Zoo.

BERENGER: I'll be brave and strong. I'll keep you safe from harm.

DAISY: You won't need to defend me, silly! We don't wish anyone any harm. And no one wishes us any, my dear.

BERENGER: Sometimes one does harm without meaning to, or rather one allows it to go unchecked. I know you didn't like poor old Mr Papillon very much – but perhaps you shouldn't have spoken to him so harshly that day when Boeuf turned into a rhinoceros. You needn't have told him he had such horny hands.

DAISY: But it was true – he had!

BERENGER: I know he had, my dear. But you could have said so less bluntly and not hurt his feelings so much. It had a big effect on him.

DAISY: Do you think so?

BERENGER: He didn't show it – he was too proud for that – but the remark certainly went home. It must have influenced his decision. Perhaps you might have been the means of saving him.

DAISY: I couldn't possibly foresee what was going to happen to him ... besides he was so ill-mannered.

BERENGER: For my own part, I shall never forgive myself for not being nicer to Jean. I never managed to give him a really solid proof of the friendship I felt for him. I wasn't sufficiently understanding with him.

DAISY: Don't worry about it. You did all you could. Nobody can do the impossible. There's no point in reproaching yourself now. Stop thinking about all those people. Forget about them. You must forget all those bad memories.

BERENGER: But they keep coming back to me. They're very real memories.

DAISY: I never knew you were such a realist – I thought you were more poetic. Where's your imagination? There are many sides to reality. Choose the one that's best for you. Escape into the world of the imagination.

BERENGER: It's easy to say that!

DAISY: Aren't I enough for you?

BERENGER: Oh yes, more than enough!

DAISY: You'll spoil everything if you go on having a bad conscience. Everybody has their faults, but you and I have got less than a lot of people.

BERENGER: Do you really think so?

DAISY: We're comparatively better than most. We're good, both of us.

BERENGER: That's true, you're good and I'm good. That's true.

DAISY: Well then we have the right to live. We even owe ourselves a duty to be happy in spite of everything. Guilt is a dangerous symptom. It shows a lack of purity.

BERENGER: You're right, it can lead to that ... [*He points to the window under which the rhinoceroses are passing and to the up-stage wall where another rhinoceros head appears.*] ... a lot of them started like that!

DAISY: We must try and not feel guilty any more.

BERENGER: How right you are, my wonderful love ... You're all my happiness; the light of my life ... We are together, aren't we? No one can separate us. Our love is the only thing that's real. Nobody has the right to stop us from being happy – in fact, nobody could, could they?

[*The telephone rings.*]

Who could that be?

DAISY [*fearful*]: Don't answer.

BERENGER: Why not?

DAISY: I don't know. I just feel it's better not to.

BERENGER: It might be Mr Papillon, or Botard, or Jean, or Dudard ringing to say they've had second thoughts. You did say it was probably only a passing phase.

DAISY: I don't think so. They wouldn't have changed their minds so quickly. They've not had time to think it over. They're bound to give it a fair trial.

BERENGER: Perhaps the authorities have decided to take action at last; maybe they're ringing to ask our help in whatever measures they've decided to adopt.

DAISY: I'd be surprised if it was them.

   [*The telephone rings again.*]

BERENGER: It is the authorities, I tell you, I recognize the ring – a long-drawn-out ring, I can't ignore an appeal from them. It can't be anyone else. [*He picks up the receiver.*] Hallo? [*Trumpetings are heard coming from the receiver.*] You hear that? Trumpeting! Listen!

   [DAISY *puts the telephone to her ear, is shocked by the sound, quickly replaces the receiver.*]

DAISY [*frightened*]: What's going on?

BERENGER: They're playing jokes now.

DAISY: Jokes in bad taste!

BERENGER: You see! What did I tell you?

DAISY: You didn't tell me anything.

BERENGER: I was expecting that; it was just what I'd predicted.

DAISY: You didn't predict anything. You never do. You can only predict things after they've happened.

BERENGER: Oh yes, I can; I can predict things all right.

DAISY: That's not nice of them – in fact it's very nasty. I don't like being made fun of.

BERENGER: They wouldn't dare make fun of you. It's me they're making fun of.

DAISY: And naturally I come in for it as well because I'm with you. They're taking their revenge. But what have we done to them?

[*The telephone rings again.*]

Pull the plug out.

BERENGER: The telephone authorities say you mustn't.

DAISY: Oh you never dare to do anything – and you say you could defend me!

BERENGER [*darting to the radio*]: Let's turn on the radio for the news!

DAISY: Yes, we must find out how things stand!

[*The sound of trumpeting comes from the radio.* BERENGER *peremptorily switches it off. But in the distance other trumpetings, like echoes, can be heard.*]

Things are getting really serious! I tell you frankly, I don't like it! [*She is trembling.*]

BERENGER [*very agitated*]: Keep calm! Keep calm!

DAISY: They've taken over the radio stations!

BERENGER [*agitated and trembling*]: Keep calm, keep calm!

[DAISY *runs to the up-stage window, then to the down-stage window and looks out;* BERENGER *does the same in the opposite order, then the two come and face each other centre-stage.*]

DAISY: It's no joke any longer. They mean business!

BERENGER: There's only them left now; nobody but them. Even the authorities have joined them.

[*They cross to the window as before, and meet again centre-stage.*]

DAISY: Not a soul left anywhere.

BERENGER: We're all alone, we're left all alone.

DAISY: That's what you wanted.

BERENGER: You mean that's what you wanted!

DAISY: It was you!

BERENGER: You!

[*Noises come from everywhere at once. Rhinoceros heads fill the up-stage wall. From left and right in the house, the noise of rushing feet and the panting breath of the animals. But all these disquieting sounds are nevertheless somehow rhythmical, making a kind of music. The loudest noises of all come from above; a noise of stamping. Plaster falls from the ceiling. The house shakes violently.*]

DAISY: The earth's trembling! [*She doesn't know where to run.*]

BERENGER: No, that's our neighbours, the Perissodactyles! [*He shakes his fist to left and right and above.*] Stop it! You're preventing us from working! Noise is forbidden in these flats! Noise is forbidden!

DAISY: They'll never listen to you!

[*However the noise does diminish, merely forming a sort of musical background.*]

BERENGER [*he, too, is afraid*]: Don't be frightened, my dear. We're together – you're happy with me, aren't you? It's enough that I'm with you, isn't it? I'll chase all your fears away.

DAISY: Perhaps it's all our own fault.

BERENGER: Don't think about it any longer. We mustn't start feeling remorse. It's dangerous to start feeling guilty. We must just live our lives, and be happy. We have the right to be happy. They're not spiteful, and we're not doing them any harm. They'll leave us in peace. You just keep calm and rest. Sit in the armchair. [*He leads her to the armchair.*] Just keep calm! [DAISY *sits in the armchair.*] Would you like a drop of brandy to pull you together?

DAISY: I've got a headache.

BERENGER [*taking up his bandage and binding Daisy's head*]: I love you, my darling. Don't you worry, they'll get over it. It's just a passing phase.

DAISY: They won't get over it. It's for good.

BERENGER: I love you. I love you madly.

DAISY [*taking off the bandage*]: Let things just take their course. What can we do about it?

BERENGER: They've all gone mad. The world is sick. They're all sick.

DAISY: We shan't be the ones to cure them.

BERENGER: How can we live in the same house with them?

DAISY [*calming down*]: We must be sensible. We must adapt ourselves and try and get on with them.

BERENGER: They can't understand us.

DAISY: They must. There's no other way.

BERENGER: Do you understand them?

DAISY: Not yet. But we must try to understand the way their minds work, and learn their language.

BERENGER: They haven't got a language! Listen ... do you call that a language?

DAISY: How do you know? You're no polyglot!

BERENGER: We'll talk about it later. We must have lunch first.

DAISY: I'm not hungry any more. It's all too much. I can't take any more.

BERENGER: But you're the strong one. You're not going to let it get you down. It's precisely for your courage that I admire you so.

DAISY: You said that before.

BERENGER: Do you feel sure of my love?

DAISY: Yes, of course.

BERENGER: I love you so.

DAISY: You keep saying the same thing, my dear.

BERENGER: Listen, Daisy, there *is* something we can do. We'll have children, and our children will have children – it'll take time, but together we can regenerate the human race.

DAISY: Regenerate the human race?

BERENGER: It happened once before.

DAISY: Ages ago. Adam and Eve ... They had a lot of courage.

BERENGER: And we, too, can have courage. We don't need all that much. It happens automatically with time and patience.

DAISY: What's the use?

BERENGER: Of course we can – with a little bit of courage.

DAISY: I don't want to have children – it's a bore.

BERENGER: How can we save the world, if you don't?

DAISY: Why bother to save it?

BERENGER: What a thing to say! Do it for me, Daisy. Let's save the world.

DAISY: After all, perhaps it's we who need saving. Perhaps we're the abnormal ones.

BERENGER: You're not yourself, Daisy, you've got a touch of fever.

DAISY: There aren't any more of our kind about anywhere, are there?

BERENGER: Daisy, you're not to talk like that!

[DAISY *looks all around at the rhinoceros heads on the walls, on the landing door, and now starting to appear along the footlights.*]

DAISY: Those are the real people. They look happy. They're content to be what they are. They don't look insane. They look very natural. They were right to do what they did.

BERENGER [*clasping his hands and looking despairingly at Daisy*]: We're the ones who are doing right, Daisy, I assure you.

DAISY: That's very presumptuous of you!

BERENGER: You know perfectly well I'm right.

DAISY: There's no such thing as absolute right. It's the world that's right – not you and me.

BERENGER: I *am* right, Daisy. And the proof is that you understand me when I speak to you.

DAISY: What does that prove?

BERENGER: The proof is that I love you as much as it's possible for a man to love a woman.

DAISY: Funny sort of argument!

BERENGER: I don't understand you any longer, Daisy. You don't know what you're saying, darling. Think of our love! Our love ...

DAISY: I feel a bit ashamed of what you call love – this morbid feeling, this male weakness. And female, too. It just doesn't compare with the ardour and the tremendous energy emanating from all these creatures around us.

BERENGER: Energy! You want some energy, do you? I can let you have some energy! [*He slaps her face.*]

DAISY: Oh! I never would have believed it possible ... [*She sinks into the armchair.*]

BERENGER: Oh forgive me, my darling, please forgive me! [*He tries to embrace her, she evades him.*] Forgive me, my darling. I didn't mean it. I don't know what came over me, losing control like that!

DAISY: It's because you've run out of arguments, that's why.

BERENGER: Oh dear! In the space of a few minutes we've gone through twenty-five years of married life.

DAISY: I pity you. I understand you all too well ...

BERENGER [*as* DAISY *weeps*]: You're probably right that I've run out of arguments. You think they're stronger than me, stronger than us. Maybe they are.

DAISY: Indeed they are.

BERENGER: Well, in spite of everything, I swear to you I'll never give in, never!

DAISY [*she rises, goes to Berenger, puts her arms round his neck*]: My poor darling, I'll help you to resist – to the very end.

BERENGER: Will you be capable of it?

DAISY: I give you my word. You can trust me.

[*The rhinoceros noises have become melodious.*]
Listen, they're singing!

BERENGER: They're not singing, they're roaring.

DAISY: They're singing.

BERENGER: They're roaring, I tell you.

DAISY: You're mad, they're singing.

BERENGER: You can't have a very musical ear, then.

DAISY: You don't know the first thing about music, poor dear – and look, they're playing as well, and dancing.

BERENGER: You call that dancing?

DAISY: It's their way of dancing. They're beautiful.

BERENGER: They're disgusting!

DAISY: You're not to say unpleasant things about them. It upsets me.

BERENGER: I'm sorry. We're not going to quarrel on their account.

DAISY: They're like gods.

BERENGER: You go too far, Daisy; take a good look at them.

DAISY: You mustn't be jealous, my dear.

[*She goes to Berenger again and tries to embrace him. This time it is* BERENGER *who frees himself.*]

BERENGER: I can see our opinions are directly opposed. It's better not to discuss the matter.

DAISY: Now you mustn't be nasty.

BERENGER: Then don't you be stupid!

DAISY [*to* BERENGER, *who turns his back on her. He looks at himself closely in the mirror*]: It's no longer possible for us to live together.

[*As* BERENGER *continues to examine himself in the mirror she goes quietly to the door, saying*]

He isn't very nice, really, he isn't very nice. [*She goes out, and is seen slowly descending the stairs.*]

BERENGER [*still looking at himself in the mirror*]: Men aren't so bad-looking, you know. And I'm not a particularly hand-some specimen! Believe me, Daisy! [*He turns round.*] Daisy! Daisy! Where are you, Daisy? You can't do that to me!

[*He darts to the door.*] Daisy! [*He gets to the landing and leans over the banister.*] Daisy! Come back! Come back, my dear! You haven't even had your lunch, Daisy, don't leave me alone! Remember your promise! Daisy! Daisy! [*He stops calling, makes a despairing gesture, and comes back into the room.*] Well, it was obvious we weren't getting along together. The home was broken up. It just wasn't working out. But she shouldn't have left like that with no explanation. [*He looks all around.*] She didn't even leave a message. That's no way to behave. Now I'm all on my own. [*He locks the door carefully, but angrily.*] But they won't get me. [*He carefully closes the windows.*] You won't get me! [*He addresses all the rhinoceros heads.*] I'm not joining you; I don't understand you! I'm staying as I am. I'm a human being. A human being. [*He sits in the armchair.*] It's an impossible situation. It's my fault she's gone. I meant everything to her. What'll become of her? That's one more person on my conscience. I can easily picture the worst, because the worst can easily happen. Poor little thing left all alone in this world of monsters! Nobody can help me find her, nobody, because there's nobody left.

[*Fresh trumpetings, hectic racings, clouds of dust.*]

I can't bear the sound of them any longer, I'm going to put cotton wool in my ears. [*He does so, and talks to himself in the mirror.*] The only solution is to convince them – but convince them of what? Are the changes reversible, that's the point? Are they reversible? It would be a labour of Hercules, far beyond me. In any case, to convince them you'd have to talk to them. And to talk to them I'd have to learn their language. Or they'd have to learn mine. But what language do I speak? What is my language? Am I talking French? Yes, it must be French. But what is French? I can call it French if I want, and nobody can say it isn't – I'm the only one who speaks it. What am I saying? Do I understand what I'm saying? Do I? [*He crosses to the middle of the room.*] And what if it's true what Daisy said, and they're the ones in the right? [*He turns back to the mirror.*] A man's not ugly to look at, not ugly at all! [*He examines himself, passing his hand over his face.*] What a funny-looking thing! What do I look like? What? [*He darts to a cupboard, takes out some photographs which he examines.*] Photographs? Who are all these people? Is it Mr Papillon – or is it Daisy? And is that Botard or Dudard or Jean? Or is it me? [*He rushes to the cupboard again and takes out two or three pictures.*] Now I recognize me: that's me, that's me! [*He hangs the pictures on the back wall, beside the rhinoceros heads.*] That's me, that's me!

[*When he hangs the pictures one sees that they are of an old man, a huge woman, and another man. The ugliness of these pictures is in contrast to the rhinoceros heads which have become very beautiful.* BERENGER *steps back to contemplate the pictures.*]

I'm not good-looking, I'm not good-looking. [*He takes down the pictures, throws them furiously to the ground, and goes over to the mirror.*] They're the good-looking ones. I was wrong! Oh, how I wish I was like them! I haven't got any horns, more's the pity! A smooth brow looks so ugly. I need one or two horns to give my sagging face a lift. Perhaps one will grow and I needn't be ashamed any more – then I could go and join them. But it will never grow! [*He looks at the palms of his hands.*] My hands are so limp – oh, why won't they get rough! [*He takes his coat off, undoes his shirt to look at his chest in the mirror.*] My skin is so slack. I can't stand this white, hairy body. Oh I'd love to have a hard skin in that wonderful dull green colour – a skin that looks decent naked without any hair on it, like theirs! [*He listens to the trumpetings.*] Their song is charming – a bit raucous perhaps, but it does have charm! I wish I could do it! [*He tries to imitate them.*] Ahh, Ahh, Brr! No, that's not it! Try again, louder! Ahh, Ahh, Brr! No, that's not it, it's too feeble, it's got no drive behind it. I'm not trumpeting at all; I'm just howling. Ahh, Ahh, Brr. There's a big difference between howling and trumpeting. I've only myself to blame; I should have gone with them while there was still time. Now it's too late! Now I'm a monster, just a monster. Now I'll never become a rhinoceros, never, never! I'm gone past changing. I want to, I really do, but I can't, I just can't. I can't stand the sight of me. I'm too ashamed! [*He turns his back on the mirror.*] I'm so ugly! People who try to hang on to their individuality always come to a bad end! [*He suddenly snaps out of it.*] Oh well, too bad! I'll take on the whole of them! I'll put up a fight against the lot of them, the whole lot of them! I'm the last man left, and I'm staying that way until the end. I'm not capitulating!

CURTAIN

THE CHAIRS

A Tragic Farce

THE CHAIRS

First produced in Paris by Sylvain Dhomme at the Théâtre Lancry, 22 April 1952.

First produced in London by Tony Richardson and performed by the English Stage Company at the Royal Court Theatre, 14 May 1957.

Characters of the Play

THE OLD MAN, *ninety-five years old*
THE OLD WOMAN, *ninety-four years old*
THE ORATOR, *forty-five to fifty years old*
And many other characters

SET: *Circular walls, with a recess at the rear of the stage. The stage is very bare. On the right, starting from the front of the stage, there are three doors. Then a window, with a stool in front of it; then another door. In the recess at the rear, a great monumental double door and two other ordinary ones, facing each other, on both sides of it; these two doors, or one of them at least, are hidden from the public. On the left of the stage, still starting from the front, there are three doors, a window with a stool right opposite the right-hand window, then a blackboard and a platform. The accompanying sketch makes the plan clearer. Centre, down-stage, there are two chairs, side by side. A gas-lamp is suspended from the ceiling.*

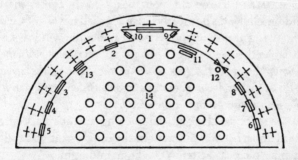

[*The curtain rises. Semi-darkness. The* OLD MAN *is standing on the stool leaning out of the left-hand window. The* OLD WOMAN *is lighting the gas-lamp. A green light. She goes and pulls the Old Man's sleeve.*]

OLD WOMAN: Hurry up, dear, and close the window. I don't like the smell of stagnant water, and the mosquitoes are coming in, too.

OLD MAN: Don't fuss!

OLD WOMAN: Come along now, dear, come and sit down. Don't lean out like that, you might fall in. You know what happened to Francis I. You must be careful.

OLD MAN: Another of your historical allusions! I'm tired of French history, my love. I want to look. The boats in the sunshine are like specks on the water.

OLD WOMAN: You can't see them, it's night-time, my pet, there is no sun.

OLD MAN: It's still casting shadows, anyway. [*He leans right out.*]

OLD WOMAN [*pulling him back with all her might*]: Ah! ... You're frightening me, my dear ... come and sit down, you won't see them coming. It's no use trying. It's dark ... [*The* OLD MAN *reluctantly lets her pull him away.*]

OLD MAN: I wanted to look. I *do* so enjoy looking at the water.

OLD WOMAN: How can you, dear? ... It makes *me* quite giddy. Oh! This house, this island, I shall never get used to it all. Water all round you ... water under the windows, water as far as the eye can see. [*The* OLD WOMAN *pulls the Old Man forward to the two chairs at the front of the stage; the* OLD MAN *sits down on the Old Woman's lap, as though it were the most natural thing in the world.*]

OLD MAN: Six o'clock in the evening and it's dark already. Remember? It was different in the old days; it was still light at nine o'clock, at ten o'clock, at midnight.

OLD WOMAN: So it was! What a memory you've got!

OLD MAN: It's all changed now.

OLD WOMAN: Do you know why it's changed?

OLD MAN: No, I don't, Semiramis, my pet. ... Perhaps, because the further we go, the deeper the rut. It's all on account of the earth, which never stops turning, turning, turning ...

OLD WOMAN: Turning, turning, my love ... [*Silence.*] Oh yes!

You really are a great scholar. You're so clever, my dear. You might have become a President General, a General Director, or even a General Physician or a Postmaster-General, if you'd wanted to, if you'd had just a little ambition in life. ...

OLD MAN: What good would that have done us? We shouldn't have had a better life ... after all, we have a job to do, I am a Quartermaster-General, since I'm a caretaker.

OLD WOMAN [*she fondles the Old Man as if he were a child*]: My little pet, angel child ...

OLD MAN: I'm so tired of everything.

OLD WOMAN: You were more cheerful when you were looking at the water. ... Just to cheer us up, let's pretend, as we did the other night.

OLD MAN: Pretend yourself, it's your turn.

OLD WOMAN: It isn't, it's yours.

OLD MAN: It isn't.

OLD WOMAN: It is.

OLD MAN: It isn't.

OLD WOMAN: It is.

OLD MAN: Semiramis, drink your tea. [*Naturally, there is no tea.*]

OLD WOMAN: Imitate February, then.

OLD MAN: I don't like the months of the year.

OLD WOMAN: There's no other kind at the moment. Go on, just to please me. ...

OLD MAN: All right, then. This is February. [*He scratches his head, like Stan Laurel.*]

OLD WOMAN [*clapping and laughing*]: Yes, that's it! Oh thank you, thank you, you really are a sweet little pet. [*She kisses him.*] You're *so* clever, you could have been at least a Post-master-General, if you'd wanted to. ...

OLD MAN: I'm a caretaker, a Quartermaster-General. [*Silence.*]

OLD WOMAN: Tell me the story. You know, *the* story: and then we arri ...

OLD MAN: What again? ... I'm tired of it ... and then we arri? That one again? You always ask me for the same thing! ... 'And then we arri ...' It's so boring. ... Every evening, every evening without exception, through seventy-five years of married life, you make me tell the same story, imitate the same people, the same months ... always the same ... let's change the subject ...

OLD WOMAN: I never get tired of it, my love ... It's *your* life, so exciting.

OLD MAN: You know it by heart.

OLD WOMAN: It's as if I forget everything straightaway ... Every evening I start with a fresh mind ... But I do, my pet, I do it on purpose, I take a purge ... I'm as good as new again, just for you, my dear, every evening ... Please hurry up and begin.

OLD MAN: All right, then.

OLD WOMAN: Come on, start telling your story ... Of course it's mine as well: what's yours is mine! Then we arri ...

OLD MAN: Then we arri ... my pet ...

OLD WOMAN: Then we arri ... my love ...

OLD MAN: Then we arrived at a great iron gate. We'd been soaked to the skin, frozen to the bone, for hours, for days, for nights, for weeks ...

OLD WOMAN: For months ...

OLD MAN: ... In the rain. ... We were chattering all over, our ears, our feet, our knees, our noses, our teeth ... that was eighty years ago now. ... They wouldn't let us in ... They might at least have opened the garden gate. [*Silence.*]

OLD WOMAN: In the garden the grass was wet.

OLD MAN: There was a path that led to a little square. And in the middle a village church. ... Where was that village? Do you remember?

OLD WOMAN: No, my dear, I've forgotten.

OLD MAN: How did we get there? Where's the road to it? I believe the place was called Paris ...

OLD WOMAN: Paris? There never was such a place, my pet.

OLD MAN: There must have been once, because it fell into ruins. ... It was the city of light and four hundred thousand years ago it faded right away ... there's nothing left of it now, except a song.

OLD WOMAN: A real song? That's funny. What is it?

OLD MAN: A lullaby, a parable: 'Paris will always be Paris.'

OLD WOMAN: Did we get there through the garden? Was it a long way?

OLD MAN [*dreamily, far away*]: The song? ... the rain? ...

OLD WOMAN: You're so clever. If you'd had just a little ambition in life, you might have become a General Editor, an Attorney-General, a General Postmaster-General ... Oh dear, all swept away under the bridge ... under the great black bridge of time ... swept away, I tell you. [*Silence.*]

OLD MAN: And then we arri ...

OLD WOMAN: Oh yes! Go on with the story ...

OLD MAN [*while the* OLD WOMAN *begins to laugh quietly, crazily, gradually working up into fits of laughter. The* OLD MAN *laughs, too*]: And then we arrived and we laughed till we cried to see the funny man arrive with his hat all awry ... it was so funny when he fell flat on his face, he had such a fat tummy ... he arrived with a case full of rice: the rice on the ground, all awry ... we laughed till we cried ... and we cried and cried ... funny fat tummy, rice on a wry face, flat on his rice, case full of face ... and we laughed till we cried ... funny hat flat on his fat face, all awry ...

OLD WOMAN [*laughing*]: ... arrived on his rice, face all awry, and we cried when we arrived, case, face, tummy, fat, rice ...

BOTH [*together, laughing*]: And then we arri. Ah! ... arri ...

arri ... Ah! ... Ah ... ri ... ri ... rice ... awry ... fat hat awry
... fat tummy funny ... rice arrived awry ... [*And then we
hear*] And then we ... fat tummy ... arri ... the case ... [*And
the* OLD COUPLE *slowly quieten down.*] Cried ... ah! ...
arrived ... ah! ... arri ... a ... wry ... rice ... face ... arri ...
va ... ris.

OLD WOMAN: So that was your famous old Paris.

OLD MAN: Parasite lost.

OLD WOMAN: Oh! you *are*, my dear, oh you *are* really, you
are *so* ... so ... you could have been something in life, much
more than a Quartermaster-General.

OLD MAN: Don't let us be boastful ... we should be satisfied
with the little we have ...

OLD WOMAN: Perhaps you've wrecked your career?

OLD MAN [*suddenly starts crying*]: Wrecked it? Dashed it to
pieces? Broken it? Oh! Where are you, mummy? Mummy,
where are you? ... hee, hee, hee, I'm an orphan. [*Groaning*]
... an orphan, a norphan ...

OLD WOMAN: Mummy's with you, what are you afraid of?

OLD MAN: No, Semiramis, my pet. You're not my mummy ...
an orphan, a norphan, who will look after me?

OLD WOMAN: But I'm still here, my love! ...

OLD MAN: That's not the same ... I want my mummy, so
there! You're not my mummy.

OLD WOMAN [*stroking him*]: You're breaking my heart.
Don't cry, little one.

OLD MAN: Hee, hee! Leave me alone; hee, hee! I feel all
cracked and smashed, I've a pain, my career is hurting me,
it's all in pieces.

OLD WOMAN: There, there!

OLD MAN [*sobbing, with his mouth wide open, like a baby*]: I'm
an orphan ... a norphan.

OLD WOMAN [*trying to coax him into being quiet*]: My little
orphan boy, you're breaking mummy's heart, my pet. [*She*

*has laready started rocking the disillusioned old man backwards
and forwards on her knees.*]

OLD MAN [*sobbing*]: Hee, hee, hee! Mummy! Where's my
mummy? I've lost my mummy.

OLD WOMAN: I'm your wife, so now I'm your mummy, too.

OLD MAN [*giving in a little*]: It's not true, I'm an orphan, hee,
hee.

OLD WOMAN [*still rocking him*]: My little sweetheart, my
little orphan, norphan, porphan, borphan, morphan.

OLD MAN [*still sulky, but coming round slowly*]: No ... I don't
want to, I wo-o-on't!

OLD WOMAN [*singing softly*]: Anorphan-lee, anorphan-lo,
anorphan-lah, anorphan-lu, anorphan-lay.

OLD MAN: No-o-o-o ... No-o-o-o.

OLD WOMAN [*as before*]: Leelo, lahlo, lulo, lay, norphan-lo,
morphan-lu, borphan-lee, porphan-lay ...

OLD MAN: Hee, hee, hee, hee. [*He sniffs and gradually calms
down.*] Where is she, my mummy?

OLD WOMAN: In the gardens of Paradise ... she can hear you,
and see you, peeping out from among the flowers; you
mustn't cry or you'll make her cry too!

OLD MAN: It's not *true* ... she *can't* see me, she *can't* hear me.
I'm an orphan, for life, and you're not my real mummy ...

OLD WOMAN [*the* OLD MAN *is almost calm now*]: There now,
you see you've nothing to worry about ... My little General's
a very clever boy ... dry those tears away, all the guests will
be here this evening and we mustn't let them see you like
this ... you haven't smashed everything, there's still some
hope left; you'll tell them all about it, you can explain it all:
You've got a message ... you're always saying you're going
to pass it on ... you must live and fight for your message ...

OLD MAN: I've a message, you're right, I must fight for it, a
mission, I can give birth to a great idea, a message for all
men, for all mankind ...

OLD WOMAN: For all mankind, my dear, your message! ...

OLD MAN: It's true, that's really true ...

OLD WOMAN [*blowing the Old Man's nose and wiping away his tears*]: That's the way! ... You're a big boy now, a real soldier, a Quartermaster-General ...

OLD MAN [*he has got off the Old Woman's knees and is trotting about excitedly*]: I'm not like other people, I've an ideal in life. I may be clever, as you say. I am quite talented, but things don't come easily to me. I've carried out my duties as Quartermaster-General satisfactorily, proved myself equal to the task, come out of it quite honourably, that ought to be enough ...

OLD WOMAN: Not for you, you're not like other men, you're greater than they are; and yet you'd have done much better if you'd got on well with everyone else, like everyone else. You quarrelled with all your friends, with all the directors, all the Generals, and with your own brother.

OLD MAN: Wasn't my fault, Semiramis, you know what he said.

OLD WOMAN: What did he say?

OLD MAN: He said: My dear friends, I've caught a flea somewhere, and I've come to see *you* in the hope of losing it again.

OLD WOMAN: Everyone says that, my love. You shouldn't have taken any notice. But why did you get upset with Carel? Was that his fault, too?

OLD MAN: You'll make me lose my temper, lose my temper. So there! Of course it was his fault. He came along one evening and this is what he said: 'Best of luck, old Kangaroo. I wish you every success and hope you get what's coming to you.' And he bellowed like a horse.

OLD WOMAN: He meant well, dear. It doesn't do to be so sensitive in life.

OLD MAN: I don't like that sort of joke.

OLD WOMAN: You could have been a General Decorator, a General in the Navy, or a General Factotum. [*A long silence. For a while they are quite motionless, sitting rigidly in their chairs.*]

OLD MAN [*dreamily*]: It was at the bottom of the bottom of the garden ... and *there* was a ... *there* was a ... *there* was a ... *what* was there, my pet?

OLD WOMAN: The city of Paris, of course!

OLD MAN: At the end, at the end of the end of the city of Paris, was, was, was what?

OLD WOMAN: Old friend, was what, old friend, was who?

OLD MAN: The place and the weather were perfect, too.

OLD WOMAN: Was the weather really so hot?

OLD MAN: What the place was like I quite forgot ...

OLD WOMAN: Forget it, then, if it worries you ...

OLD MAN: It's too far away, I can't, I can't ... bring it back ... where was it?

OLD WOMAN: Was what?

OLD MAN: What I ... What you ... where was it? and who?

OLD WOMAN: Wherever it was, whatever it was, I'd come with you, old friend, to the end, I'd follow you.

OLD MAN: Ah! I find it so difficult to express myself ... and I *must* tell everything, too.

OLD WOMAN: It's your sacred duty. You haven't the right to keep your message to yourself; you must reveal it to mankind, everyone's waiting for it ... the whole universe is waiting just for you.

OLD MAN: Yes, yes, I'll do it.

OLD WOMAN: You've really decided? You must.

OLD MAN: Drink your tea.

OLD WOMAN: You might have been an Orator-General, if you'd had a little more will-power in life ... I am proud and happy to hear that at last you've decided to speak to all the countries of Europe, to all the continents in the world!

OLD MAN: But I find it so difficult to express myself; things don't come easily to me.

OLD WOMAN: Once you begin, things come easily enough, like life and death ... you just have to make up your mind. It's as we speak that we find our ideas, our words, ourselves, too, in our own words, and the city, the garden, perhaps everything comes back and we're not orphans any more.

OLD MAN: I shan't do the talking myself, I've engaged a professional orator to speak in my name, you'll see.

OLD WOMAN: So it's really going to be this evening? I suppose you've invited everybody? All the important people, all the property-owners and all the scientists?

OLD MAN: Yes, all the learned and the landed. [Silence.]

OLD WOMAN: The wardens? the bishops? the chemists? the boiler-makers? the violinists? the shop-stewards? the presidents? the constables? the tradesmen? the public buildings? the penholders? the chromosomes?

OLD MAN: Yes, yes, and the postmen, the typists, and the artists, anyone who could be called a scientist or a property-owner.

OLD WOMAN: And the bankers?

OLD MAN: I've invited *them*.

OLD WOMAN: The proletarians? the parliamentarians? the functionaries? the reactionaries? the revolutionaries? the mental specialists and the mental patients?

OLD MAN: All of them, of course, all of them; they're all scientists and property-owners.

OLD WOMAN: Don't get so angry, my love. I didn't mean to upset you, but like all men of genius you are so forgetful; this meeting's important, they must come this evening, all of them. Are you sure they will? Did they promise?

OLD MAN: Drink your tea, Semiramis. [Silence.]

OLD WOMAN: The Pope, the popinjays, and the papers?

OLD MAN: I've invited them too. [Silence.] I shall deliver

them my message ... All my life I felt I was suffocating; and
now they'll know everything, thanks to you and the Orator,
the only people who have understood me.

OLD WOMAN: I'm so proud of you ...

OLD MAN: The meeting will soon be starting.

OLD WOMAN: So it's really true, they're going to come this
evening? You won't want to cry any more. When we've
got scientists and property-owners, we don't need daddies
and mummies. [*Silence.*] We couldn't put the meeting off
now. I hope it doesn't make us too tired! [*The excitement is
mounting. The* OLD MAN *has already started trotting round the
Old Woman, with short, uncertain steps, like a child's or a very
old man's. He has already succeeded in taking a few steps towards
one of the doors, but has come back to go round her again.*]

OLD MAN: You really think we shall find it tiring?

OLD WOMAN: You *have* got a bit of a cold.

OLD MAN: How could we postpone it?

OLD WOMAN: Let's invite them for another evening. You
could telephone them.

OLD MAN: Don't be silly. I can't, it's too late. They must be
on the boats by now!

OLD WOMAN: You oughtn't to have been so rash. [*A boat
can be heard slipping through the water.*]

OLD MAN: I believe that's someone already ... [*The noise gets
louder.*] ... Yes, someone's coming! ... [*The* OLD WOMAN
gets up too and hobbles about.]

OLD WOMAN: Perhaps it's the Orator.

OLD MAN: He wouldn't be in such a hurry. It must be someone else. [*A bell rings.*] Ah!

OLD WOMAN: Ah! [*Nervously the* OLD COUPLE *make for
the concealed door back-stage right. As they move, they go on
talking.*]

OLD MAN: Come along ...

OLD WOMAN: I haven't combed my hair ... wait a moment ...

[*She tidies her hair and straightens her dress as she hobbles along, pulling up her thick red stockings.*]

OLD MAN: You ought to have got ready before ... you had plenty of time.

OLD WOMAN: What a sight I look ... such an old frock on, all creased up ...

OLD MAN: You'd only got to iron it ... hurry up! You're keeping people waiting. [*The* OLD MAN *reaches the door in the recess, followed by the grumbling* OLD WOMAN; *for a moment they disappear from sight; they can be heard opening the door and then shutting it again, as they let someone in.*]

OLD WOMAN'S VOICE: Good morning, Madam, very pleased to make your acquaintance. Be careful, don't spoil your hat. You can take out the hat-pin, you'll feel more comfortable. Oh no! No one will sit on it.

OLD MAN'S VOICE: Put your fur down there. Let me help you. No, it will come to no harm.

OLD WOMAN'S VOICE: Oh, what a pretty suit ... a blouse in red, white, and blue ... You will have some biscuits, won't you? ... But you're not fat ... no ... just plump ... Do put your umbrella down.

OLD MAN'S VOICE: Will you come this way, please?

OLD MAN [*his back to the audience*]: My job is a very ordinary one ... [*The* OLD COUPLE *turn to face the audience at the same time, moving a little apart to leave room for the Lady Guest between them. She is invisible. The* OLD COUPLE *now come forward to the front of the stage, as they talk to the invisible Lady between them.*]

OLD MAN [*to the invisible Lady*]: Have you been having good weather?

OLD WOMAN [*to the invisible Lady*]: You're not feeling too tired? ... A little, perhaps.

OLD MAN [*to the invisible Lady*]: At the seaside ...

OLD WOMAN [*to the invisible Lady*]: Really most kind of you.

OLD MAN [to the invisible Lady]: I'll bring you a chair. [The OLD MAN goes off left, through Door No. 6.]

OLD WOMAN [to the invisible Lady]: Meanwhile, why don't you sit here? [She points to one of the two chairs and sits down on the other one, on the right of the invisible Lady.] What a pretty fan! My husband ... [The OLD MAN reappears through Door No. 7, carrying a chair.] ... gave me one something like it, seventy-three years ago ... I still have it ... [The OLD MAN sets the chair down to the left of the invisible Lady.] ... it was a birthday present! ... [The OLD MAN sits down on the chair he has just brought, so that the invisible Lady is in the middle. The OLD MAN looks at the Lady, smiles at her, nods his head, rubs his hands gently together, and appears to be following what she is saying. The OLD WOMAN does the same.]

OLD MAN: Madam, the cost of living has always been high.

OLD WOMAN [to the Lady]: You're quite right ... [The Lady speaks.] I agree with you. It's time there was a change ... [In a different tone of voice] My husband may be having something to do with it ... he will tell you.

OLD MAN [to the Old Woman]: Ssh! Be quiet, Semiramis, it's not time to talk about it yet. [To the Lady] Forgive me, Madam, for rousing your curiosity. [The Lady reacts to this.] Dear Lady, please don't insist ... [The OLD COUPLE smile. They even laugh. They look as if they are enjoying the story the Lady is telling. A pause: a lull in the conversation. Their faces have lost all expression.]

OLD MAN [to the Lady]: Oh yes, you're perfectly right ...

OLD WOMAN: Yes, yes, yes ... Oh, but no!

OLD MAN: Yes, yes, yes. By all means.

OLD WOMAN: Yes?

OLD MAN: No!?

OLD WOMAN: You've said it.

OLD MAN [laughing]: It can't be true!

OLD WOMAN [*to invisible Lady*]: Oh, I see! [*To the Old Man*] She's delightful.

OLD MAN [*to Old Woman*]: The lady's made a conquest, has she! [*To the Lady*] Well done!

OLD WOMAN [*to the Lady*]: You're not like the young people of today ...

OLD MAN [*he is painfully bending down to pick up an invisible object that the invisible Lady has dropped*]: No, please ... please don't trouble yourself ... I'll pick it up ... There now! You're quicker than I am ... [*He straightens up.*]

OLD WOMAN [*to the Old Man*]: She's younger than you are!

OLD MAN [*to the Lady*]: Old age is a terrible burden. I wish I could grant you Eternal Youth.

OLD WOMAN [*to the Lady*]: He really means that, it comes straight from his heart. [*To the Old Man*] My pet! [*Silence for a few moments. The* OLD COUPLE *look at the Lady, their faces seen in profile, and smile politely; then they look towards the audience, and back again to the Lady, smiling in response to her smile; then they answer her questions with the following replies.*]

OLD WOMAN: Most kind of you to take such an interest in us.

OLD MAN: We live a very retired life.

OLD WOMAN: He's not a misanthropist, but my husband likes peace and quiet.

OLD MAN: We have the wireless, I go fishing, and then there's quite a regular ferry service.

OLD WOMAN: There are two boats every Sunday morning and one in the evening, not to speak of the privately-owned ones.

OLD MAN: When the weather's fine, there's a moon.

OLD WOMAN: He still carries out his duties as Quartermaster-General ... it *does* keep him busy ... That's true, at his age he could take a little rest.

OLD MAN: I shall have plenty of time for rest when I'm in my grave.

OLD WOMAN [*to the Old Man*]: Oh, don't say that, my love!
[*To the Lady*] The family, what's left of it, and my husband's
old friends, still used to come and see us from time to time,
ten years ago ...

OLD MAN [*to the Lady*]: In the winter, a good book, sitting
by the stove, the memories of a life-time ...

OLD WOMAN [*to the Lady*]: A simple life, but a full one ... two
hours every day he works at his message. [*A bell rings. The
sound of an approaching boat has already been heard.*]

OLD WOMAN [*to the Old Man*]: Somebody there. Go quickly.

OLD MAN [*to the Lady*]: Will you excuse me, Madam? I
shan't be a moment! [*To the Old Woman*] Quick! Go and
fetch some chairs! [*Someone is pulling the bell furiously.*]

OLD MAN [*in great haste, very tottery, goes to the door on the right;
while the* OLD WOMAN *does her best to hobble quickly to the
concealed door on the left*]: Sounds like someone used to giving
orders. [*He hurries to open Door No. 2; the invisible Colonel
comes in; perhaps it would be a good idea if one could hear,
discreetly, a few blasts on a trumpet, a few notes of 'The Colonel's
Salute'; as soon as he opens the door, the* OLD MAN *freezes into
a respectful position of attention.*] Ah! ... Colonel! [*He raises
his arm vaguely in the direction of his forehead for a salute that
is barely recognizable.*] Good evening, Colonel! ... This is
indeed an amazing honour for me ... I ... I never expected ...
although ... and yet ... well I'm very proud to see you in my
humble abode, such a distinguished hero ... [*He shakes an
invisible hand, held out by the invisible Colonel, bows ceremoniously, and then straightens up.*] Nevertheless, without
false modesty, may I confess that I do not feel myself entirely
unworthy of your visit! Proud, yes ... but not unworthy... !
[*The* OLD WOMAN *appears with a chair, from the right.*]

OLD WOMAN: Oh! What a fine uniform! What pretty
decorations! Who is he, my love?

OLD MAN [*to the Old Woman*]: Can't you see it's the Colonel?

OLD WOMAN [*to the Old Man*]: Ah!

OLD MAN [*to the Old Woman*]: Count the pips! [*To the Colonel*] My wife, Semiramis. [*To the Old Woman*] Come and be introduced to the Colonel. [*The* OLD WOMAN *comes forward, dragging her chair with her, and makes a curtsey without letting go of it. To the Colonel*] My wife. [*To the Old Woman*] The Colonel.

OLD WOMAN: So pleased to meet you. A most welcome guest. You are an old friend of my husband's, he's a General ...

OLD MAN [*displeased*]: Quartermaster, quartermaster ...

OLD WOMAN [*the invisible Colonel kisses the Old Woman's hand; this is obvious from the* OLD WOMAN'S *gesture of raising her hand as though to his lips; the* OLD WOMAN *lets the chair fall in her confusion*]: Oh! What a polite man ... anyone can see he's out of the ordinary, really superior! ... [*She picks up the chair again; to the Colonel*] This chair is for you ...

OLD MAN [*to the invisible Colonel*]: I beg you to follow us, Sir ... [*They all move forward, the* OLD WOMAN *dragging her chair; to the Colonel*] Yes, there is someone else here. We're expecting a large number of guests! ...

[*The* OLD WOMAN *places her chair on the right.*]

OLD WOMAN [*to the Colonel*]: Please take a seat. [*The* OLD MAN *introduces the two invisible characters.*]

OLD MAN: A young lady of our acquaintance ...

OLD WOMAN: A very good friend of ours ... renowned in military circles.

OLD MAN [*as before*]: The Colonel ...

OLD WOMAN [*indicating the chair she has just brought up for the Colonel*]: Do take this chair ...

OLD MAN [*to the Old Woman*]: No, no, can't you see the Colonel wants to sit next to the Lady! ... [*The Colonel sits down invisibly on the third chair from the left; the invisible Lady is assumed to be on the second one; an inaudible conversation*

*starts up between the two invisible characters sitting next to each
other; the* OLD COUPLE *remain standing behind their chairs, on
either side of the two invisible guests: the* OLD MAN *on the left,
beside the Lady, the* OLD WOMAN *on the right, beside the
Colonel.*]

OLD WOMAN [*listening to the conversation between the guests*]:
Oh! Oh! that's going a bit too far.

OLD MAN: Perhaps. [*The* OLD MAN *and the* OLD WOMAN
*now make signs to each other, above the heads of the two guests,
as they listen to the conversation, which seems to have taken a
turn that displeases the* OLD COUPLE. *Suddenly*] Yes, Sir,
they haven't arrived yet, but they're coming. The Orator
will be speaking on my behalf, he will explain what my
message means ... Colonel, I really ought to warn you that
this lady's husband may be here at any moment.

OLD WOMAN [*to the Old Man*]: Who is this gentleman?

OLD MAN [*to the Old Woman*]: I've told you, it's the Colonel.
[*Invisibly, something not quite respectable is happening.*]

OLD WOMAN [*to the Old Man*]: I knew it.

OLD MAN: Why did you ask me then?

OLD WOMAN: To find out. Your cigarette, Colonel, not on
the floor, please!

OLD MAN: Please, Colonel, I've forgotten, Sir. The last war,
did you lose it or win it?

OLD WOMAN [*to the invisible Lady*]: But, my dear girl, you
can't let him treat you like this!

OLD MAN [*to the Colonel*]: Take a good look at me, Sir! Don't
I look like a real soldier? Once, Colonel, during a battle ...

OLD WOMAN: That's going much too far! It's not nice!
[*Pulling at the Colonel's invisible sleeve*] Listen to what he's
saying now. Do something to stop him, my love!

OLD MAN [*going quickly on with his story*]: All by myself I
accounted for 209; that's what we called them, they jumped
so high in the air trying to escape, though they weren't

quite as thick as flies, not so much fun, of course, Colonel, but thanks to my strength of mind, I killed them ... Oh no! No, please stop it!

OLD WOMAN [to the Colonel]: My husband never tells a lie: I know we're very old, but we are respectable people.

OLD MAN [forcefully to the Colonel]: If a man wants to be a proper hero, he must have good manners, too!

OLD WOMAN [to the Colonel]: I've known you for a long time now, and I should never have thought it of you. [To the Lady, as more boats are heard] I should never have thought it of him. We do have our self-respect, our own personal dignity.

OLD MAN [in a very quavering voice]: I'm not past the age when I can carry arms yet. [Bell rings.] Excuse me, I must open the door. [He makes a clumsy movement and the Lady's chair is upset.] I beg your pardon.

OLD WOMAN [rushing forward]: You haven't hurt yourself? [The OLD COUPLE help the invisible Lady to her feet.] Now you're all dirty, look at the dust. [She helps to dust the Lady down. Bell rings again.]

OLD MAN: I'm so sorry. Please forgive me. [To the Old Woman] Go and bring a chair.

OLD WOMAN [to the two invisible Guests]: Please excuse us a moment. [As the OLD MAN goes to open Door No. 3, the OLD WOMAN goes out through Door No. 5 to look for a chair, and will come back through Door No. 8.]

OLD MAN [as he makes for the door]: He wanted to put me in a rage. I almost feel cross with him. [He opens the door.] Why, it's you, Madam! I can hardly believe my own eyes, and yet I ... I really wasn't expecting you ... really it's ... Oh, how can you say that. ... When I've been thinking about you all my life, all my life, Madam, you were known as the Lovely Miss ... so this is your husband ... I did not hear about it, of course ... you haven't changed at all ... yes, perhaps you're right, your nose really has got longer, it's filled out, too ... I didn't notice it at first, but now I can see ... terribly long ... ah! what a pity! But you didn't do it on purpose ... how did it happen, then? ... I see, very gradually ... oh, I'm sorry, Sir, may I call you a dear friend of mine? You see I knew your wife a long time before you did ... oh yes, just the same person, but with quite a different nose ... my congratulations, Sir, you seem to be very much in love.

[*The* OLD WOMAN *appears through Door No. 8 with a chair.*]

Semiramis, *two* people have arrived, so we need another chair ...

[*The* OLD WOMAN *sets her chair down behind the other four, then goes out through Door No. 8 to come back through Door No. 5 a few minutes later, carrying another chair, which she sets down beside the last one. By then the* OLD MAN *should have brought his guests to her side.*]

Do please come and be introduced to the other guests ... now then, Madam ... oh! lovely, lovely Miss Lovely, that's what you were called ... you're nearly bent double now ... oh! yes, Sir, she's still very lovely, all the same; such pretty eyes behind those spectacles; her hair is white, of course, but behind the white hairs, there are brown ones and blue ones, I'm sure there are ... This way please ... What's this, a present, Sir? For my wife? [*To the Old Woman, who has just arrived with the chair*] Semiramis, this is the lovely, you know, the lovely ... [*To the Colonel and the first invisible Lady*] This is Miss, I beg your pardon, Mrs Lovely, don't smile ... and her husband ... [*To the Old Woman*] A friend of my childhood days, I've often told you about her ... and her husband. [*To the invisible Colonel and the first Lady again*] And her husband ...

OLD WOMAN [*curtseying*]: Most distinguished. A fine figure of a man, I must say. How do you do, how do you do.

[*With a wave of the hand in the direction of the first guests*]
Friends of ours, yes ...

OLD MAN [*to the Old Woman*]: He's just brought you a present. [*The* OLD WOMAN *takes the present.*]

OLD WOMAN: Oh dear! Is it a flower? Or a cradle? A peartree? Or a pheasant?

OLD MAN [*to the Old Woman*]: No, no. Can't you see it's a picture? It doesn't matter what it's meant to represent.

OLD WOMAN: Oh yes! Very pleasant! Thank you so much ... [*To the first invisible Lady*] Would you like to see it, dear?

OLD MAN [*to the invisible Colonel*]: Would you like to see it?

OLD WOMAN [*to Mrs Lovely's husband*]: Oh, Doctor, Doctor! I often feel sick, feel hot all over, get cold feet and a cold in the head, have pains and chilblains and wind round my heart, Doctor, Doctor! ...

OLD MAN [*to the Old Woman*]: This gentleman is not a doctor, he's a photographer.

OLD WOMAN [*to the first Lady*]: If you've had a good look at it, you can hang it up. [*To Old Man*] I don't mind, he's a charming man anyway, quite devastating. [*To the Photographer*] I'm not trying to pay you compliments, but ... [*The* OLD COUPLE *should now be behind the chairs, very close to each other, almost touching, but back to back: they are both talking; the* OLD MAN *to Mrs Lovely, the* OLD WOMAN *to the Photographer. Every now and again they turn their heads to address a remark to one of the first guests.*]

OLD MAN [*to Mrs Lovely*]: I'm quite overwhelmed ... You really are you, after all ... I was in love with you a hundred years ago ... there's been such a great change in you ... there's been no change in you at all ... I was in love with you then, I love you now ...

OLD WOMAN [*to the Photographer*]: Oh! Really, Sir! ...

OLD MAN [*to the Colonel*]: I quite agree with you there.

OLD WOMAN [*to the Photographer*]: Oh, really, Sir, really! ...

[*To the first Lady*] Thank you for hanging it up ... I'm sorry to have disturbed you.

[*The lighting is stronger now. It goes on getting stronger and stronger as more of the invisible guests arrive.*]

OLD MAN [*almost snivelling, to Mrs Lovely*]: Where are the snows of yesteryear?

OLD WOMAN [*to the Photographer*]: Oh, really! Really! ... Really! Really! ...

OLD MAN [*pointing the first Lady out to Mrs Lovely*]: A young friend of ours ... a very sweet girl ...

OLD WOMAN [*pointing the Colonel out to the Photographer*]: Yes, he's a Colonel in the Civil Service, cavalry ... an old friend of my husband's ... a subordinate, my husband's a General ...

OLD MAN [*to Mrs Lovely*]: Your ears weren't always so pointed! ... do you remember, my lovely?

OLD WOMAN [*to the Photographer, mincing grotesquely. She should become more coquettish as the scene goes on: showing her thick red stockings, lifting her numerous skirts, revealing a petticoat full of holes, uncovering her ancient breasts; then, throwing her head back, hands on hips, uttering erotic cries, thrusting her pelvis forward, standing with legs apart, she laughs like an old whore. This aspect of the OLD WOMAN is quite different from anything we have seen up to now or are to see later; it should suggest something in the OLD WOMAN'S character that normally remains hidden and it vanishes abruptly.*] I'm too old for that now ... you don't think so?

OLD MAN [*to Mrs Lovely, romantically*]: When we were young, the moon was a living planet; ah! yes, yes, if we had dared, but we were only children. Would you like to live those long-lost days again ... can we go back? Can we go back? Oh, no! no! It's too late now. Time has raced past us like a train. It has left its lines in our skin. Do you think plastic surgery can work miracles? [*To the Colonel*] I am a

soldier, and so are you; soldiers are always young, generals
are like gods ... [*To Mrs Lovely*] That's how it ought to be ...
But alas! We have lost everything. We could have been so
happy, I tell you; perhaps there are flowers coming up
through the snow! ...

OLD WOMAN [*to the Photographer*]: Flatterer! Naughty boy!
Aah! I look young for my age? You're a dashing little
dago, a really exciting man.

OLD MAN [*to Mrs Lovely*]: May I play Tristan to your Isolde?
Beauty lies in the heart ... you see, we could have had our
share of bliss, beauty and eternity ... eternity ... Why didn't
we dare? We didn't want it enough ... now ... everything
is lost to us, lost, lost, lost.

OLD WOMAN [*to the Photographer*]: Oh no! Oh! No, oh! La,
la! I'm trembling all over. Are you tickled, too? A tickler
or just ticklish? I really shouldn't ... [*She laughs*] Do you like
my petticoat? Or do you prefer the skirt?

OLD MAN [*to Mrs Lovely*]: It's a wretched life, a Quartermaster-General's!

OLD WOMAN [*looking towards the first invisible Lady*]: How do
you make *crêpes de Chine*? The egg of an ox, an hour of
flour, and some gastric juices. [*To the Photographer*] You've
got very feeling fingers, ah! ... well, I mean to s-a-a-y! ...
oh-oh-oh-oh!

OLD MAN [*to Mrs Lovely*]: My worthy spouse, Semiramis, has
taken the place of my mother. [*He turns to the Colonel.*] But,
Colonel, I told you that before: Truth is where you find it.
[*He turns back to Mrs Lovely.*]

OLD WOMAN [*to the Photographer*]: You really, really believe
you can have children at any age? children *of* any age?

OLD MAN [*to Mrs Lovely*]: That's exactly what saved me: the
inner life, a quiet home, austerity, my scientific research,
philosophy, my message ...

OLD WOMAN [*to the Photographer*]: I've never been unfaithful to my husband the General ... not so hard! You'll have me on the floor ... I'm only his poor old mother! [*She starts sobbing.*] A grand, great, grand [*She repulses him.*] great ... mother. It's my conscience that's protesting like this. For me, the branch of the apple-tree is broken. You must ask someone else to show you the way. I don't want to gather life's roses ...

OLD MAN [*to Mrs Lovely*]: ... preoccupations of a nobler kind ... [*The OLD COUPLE lead Mrs Lovely and the Photographer up to the other two invisible guests, and bid them sit down.*]

OLD COUPLE [*to the Photographer and Mrs Lovely*]: Sit down, sit down, please.

[*The OLD PAIR sit down, he on the left, she on the right, with the four empty chairs between them. A long scene that is almost silent, except for an occasional Yes or No. The OLD COUPLE are listening to what the invisible guests are saying.*]

OLD WOMAN [*to the Photographer*]: We've had one son ... still alive, of course ... he went away ... It's the usual story ... a bit strange perhaps ... he left his parents ... had a heart of gold ... a very long time ago ... And we loved him so much he slammed the door ... My husband and I struggled with him to try and stop him going ... he was seven years old, the age of discretion. We called after him: My son, my child, my son, my child ... and he never looked round ...

OLD MAN: No ... no ... I'm sorry to say we never had children ... I should have liked a son ... so would Semiramis ... we did what we could ... poor Semiramis, she's such a motherly woman. Perhaps it was better that way. I myself was an ungrateful child ... Oh dear! ... Grief, regrets, and remorse, that's all there is ... all that's left ...

OLD WOMAN: He used to say: You kill the birds! Why do you kill the birds? ... We don't kill birds ... we've never hurt a fly ... His eyes were full of tears. He wouldn't let us wipe them away. He wouldn't let us near them. He would say: Yes, you do, you kill all the birds, all the birds ... and he would wave his little fists at us ... You're telling lies, you're trying to deceive me! The streets are full of the birds you've killed and the little children dying. Can't you hear the birds singing? ... No, I can only hear moaning and groaning. The sky is red with blood ... No, my child, the sky is blue ... And again he would cry: You've deceived me, and I loved you so much, I thought you were good ... the streets are full of dead birds, you've put out their eyes ... Daddy, mummy, you're wicked, wicked! ... I won't stay with you any more ... I threw myself at his feet ... His father was weeping. But we couldn't hold him back ... We could still hear him shouting: It's all your fault ... but what does that mean?

OLD MAN: I left my mother to die all alone in a ditch. She called after me, crying feebly: My little boy, my beloved child, don't leave me to die all alone ... Stay with me. I'm not long for this world. Don't worry, mother, I said, I'll soon be back. I was in a hurry ... I was going to a dance. I'll be back soon. When I did come back, she was dead and buried deep in the ground. I started digging to try and find her ... but I couldn't. ... I know, I know it always happens, sons leaving their mothers and as good as killing their fathers ... Life is like that. ... but it tortures me ... the others don't mind ...

OLD WOMAN: He shouted: Daddy, mummy, I shall never see you again ...

OLD MAN: It tortures me, yes, but not the others ...

OLD WOMAN: Don't talk to my husband about him. *He* was so fond of *his* parents. He never left them for a moment. He looked after them, spoiled them even ... They died in his arms and these were their last words: You have been a wonderful son to us. God will be kind to you.

OLD MAN: I can still see her lying in that ditch and in her hand there was a lily of the valley, and she cried out: Remember me, remember me ... her eyes were full of tears, and she called me by the nickname I had as a child: Little chick, she said, little chick, don't leave me here all alone.

OLD WOMAN [to the Photographer]: He's never written to us. Now and again a friend tells us he's seen him here or there, that he's well, that he's made a good husband ...

OLD MAN [to Mrs Lovely]: She'd been in her grave a long time, when I came back. [To the first Lady] Oh, but there is, Madam! There's a cinema in the house, and a restaurant, and bathrooms ...

OLD WOMAN [to the Colonel]: Why, yes, Colonel, it's just because he ...

OLD MAN: When you come to think of it, that's all it really is. [A very broken conversation, slowly coming to a stop.]

OLD WOMAN: So long as!

OLD MAN: So I didn't ... told him ... Naturally ...

OLD WOMAN [dialogue completely disconnected, run right down]: Well ...

OLD MAN: To our and to theirs.

OLD WOMAN: To what.

OLD MAN: I to him.

OLD WOMAN: Him, or her?

OLD MAN: Them.

OLD WOMAN: Peppermints ... You don't say.

OLD MAN: There aren't.

OLD WOMAN: Why?

OLD MAN: Yes.

OLD WOMAN: I.

OLD MAN: Well.

OLD WOMAN: Well.

OLD MAN [to the first Lady]: Beg pardon, Madam?
   [A long silence, the old pair motionless on their chairs. Then the bell rings again.]

OLD MAN [*with an excitement that goes on increasing*]: They're coming. People. More people.

OLD WOMAN: I thought I could hear some boats ...

OLD MAN: I'll go and open the door. Fetch some chairs. Please excuse me, ladies and gentlemen. [*He moves towards Door No. 7.*]

OLD WOMAN [*to the invisible guests who are already there*]: Please stand up for a moment. The Orator should be coming soon. I must get the room ready for the lecture. [*The OLD WOMAN arranges the chairs, their backs towards the audience.*] Would you mind helping me? Thank you.

OLD MAN [*opening Door No. 7*]: Good evening, Gentlemen. Will you kindly come in? [*The three or four invisible people who arrive are very tall, and the OLD MAN has to stand on tiptoe to shake hands with them. The OLD WOMAN follows the OLD MAN when she has arranged the chairs as described above.*]

OLD MAN [*introducing everyone*]: My wife ... Mr ... Mrs ... my wife ... Mr ... Mrs ... my wife ...

OLD WOMAN: Who are all these people, my love?

OLD MAN: Go and fetch some chairs, dear.

OLD WOMAN: I can't see to everything ! ... [*She goes out, grumbling, through Door No. 7, while the OLD MAN brings the new arrivals to the front of the stage.*]

OLD MAN: Mind you don't drop your cine-camera ... [*More introductions*] The Colonel ... the Lady ... Mrs Lovely ... The Photographer ... Here are the journalists, they've come to listen to the lecture too; he's sure to be here soon ... Don't get impatient ... you won't be bored ... with all of you together ...

[*The OLD WOMAN makes her appearance through Door No. 7, carrying two chairs.*]

Hurry up, there, a little quicker with those chairs ... we need one more.

[*The OLD WOMAN goes off, grumbling still, to look for*

another through Door No. 3 and comes back through Door No. 8.]

OLD WOMAN: All right, all right ... I'm doing my best ... I'm not a machine ... Who are all these people? [*She goes out.*]

OLD MAN: Please sit down, the ladies with the ladies, the gentlemen with the gentlemen, or the other way round, if you prefer ... We haven't any better chairs ... it's all rather improvised ... so sorry ... take the one in the middle ... do you need a pen? ... phone 'Maillot' and you'll get Monique ... Claude is 'Providence' ... I haven't got a wireless ... Yes, I take all the newspapers ... it depends on a number of things; I look after the lodgings, but I have no staff ... I have to economize, you know ... *please*, no interviews, not just now ... we'll see afterwards ... there'll be a seat for you in just a moment ... but what can she be doing? ...

[*The* OLD WOMAN *appears through Door No. 8 with a chair.*] Faster, Semiramis ...

OLD WOMAN: I'm doing my best ... Who are all these people?

OLD MAN: I'll tell you later.

OLD WOMAN: And that woman, my love? Who's that girl?

OLD MAN: Don't worry about her ... [*To the Colonel*] Don't you think, Colonel, that journalism, as a profession, is rather like a warrior's? ... [*To the Old Woman*] Look after the ladies, my dear ... [*The bell rings. The* OLD MAN *rushes to Door No. 8.*] I'm coming, wait a minute ... [*To the* OLD WOMAN] What about those chairs!

OLD WOMAN: Forgive me, ladies and gentlemen, if I ... [*She goes out through Door No. 3 to come back through Door No. 2; the* OLD MAN *goes to open the concealed door, Door No. 9, and disappears just as the* OLD WOMAN *comes back through Door No. 3.*]

OLD MAN [*hidden from view*]: Come in ... come in ... come in ... come in ... [*He reappears, leading in a large number of people, among them a very small child, whose hand he is holding.*] Nobody should bring a small child to a lecture on science ... the poor little chap'll be bored to tears ... it'll be a fine thing if he starts screaming and wets all the ladies' dresses! [*He leads them to the centre of the stage; the* OLD WOMAN *arrives with two chairs.*] May I introduce my wife, Semiramis; these are their children.

OLD WOMAN: Ladies, Gentlemen ... Oh! Aren't they little dears!

OLD MAN: That one is the youngest.

OLD WOMAN: Isn't he sweet ... sweet ... really sweet!

OLD MAN: There aren't enough chairs.

OLD WOMAN: Oh dear oh dear oh dear oh dear ... [*She goes out to find another chair; from now on she will go out and come in through Doors No. 2 and 3, on the right.*]

OLD MAN: Take the little one on your lap ... the twins can use the same chair. Be careful, it's not a very strong one ... these chairs belong to the house, they're the owner's. Yes, children, you're right, he'll be cross with us, he's a nasty man ... He'd like us to buy them, but they're not worth the money.

   [*The* OLD WOMAN *comes up with another chair, as fast as she can.*]

You don't all know each other, do you? ... it's the first time you've met ... but you used to know each other by name ... [*To the Old Woman*] Semiramis, help me to introduce everyone....

OLD WOMAN: Who are all these people? ... May I introduce – allow me, may I introduce ... but who are they?

OLD MAN: May I introduce you to ... troduce you to ... introduce you to her ... Mr, Mrs, Miss ... Mr ... Mrs ... Mrs ... Mr ...

OLD WOMAN [*to the Old Man*]: Did you put your pullover on? [*To the invisible guests*] Mr, Mrs, Mr ... [*Bell rings again.*]

OLD MAN: People! [*Bell rings again.*]

OLD WOMAN: People!

[*Bell rings again, then again, and again. The* OLD MAN *is overwhelmed; the chairs, the backs turned to the audience so that they face the platform, are lined up in straight rows, as though arranged for a show, and grow more and more numerous; the* OLD MAN, *out of breath and mopping his brow, goes from one door to the next and seats the invisible people, while the* OLD WOMAN, *absolutely exhausted, clippity-clops as fast as she can from door to door, fetching and carrying chairs. There are now vast numbers of invisible people on the stage; the* OLD COUPLE *have to take care not to bump into them, and must pick their way through the rows of chairs. The movements could be arranged as follows: The* OLD MAN *goes to Door No. 4, the* OLD WOMAN *goes out through Door No. 3 and comes back through Door No. 2; the* OLD MAN *goes to open Door No. 7, the* OLD WOMAN *goes out through Door No. 8 and comes back through Door No. 6 with the chairs, etc., so that they go right round the stage, using all the doors.*]

OLD WOMAN: Excuse me ... sorry ... what ... right ... sorry ... excuse me ...

OLD MAN: Gentlemen ... come in ... Ladies ... come in ... it's you, Madam ... allow me ... yes ...

OLD WOMAN [*with the chairs*]: There ... and there ... too many people ... there are really too many ... too many, really, ah! there there there there. ...

[*From outside the noise of the boats on the water can be heard growing louder and nearer; all the noises off now come only from the wings. The* OLD COUPLE *go on executing the movements indicated above; doors are opened, chairs are brought in. The bell rings and rings.*]

OLD MAN: This table's in the way. [*He moves it, or rather he appears to be moving a table, in such a way as not to slow the action down, the* OLD WOMAN *helping him.*] There's hardly enough room here, please excuse us ...

OLD WOMAN [*as she pretends to be helping the* OLD MAN *to move the table*]: Did you put your pullover on?
   [*Bell rings.*]

OLD MAN: More people! More chairs! People! Chairs! Come in, come in, Ladies, Gentlemen ... Faster, Semiramis ... I'd help you if I could ...

OLD WOMAN: Excuse me ... so sorry ... good evening, Madam ... Madam ... Sir ... Sir ... yes, yes, the chairs ...

OLD MAN [*while the sound of the bell grows louder and louder and the noise of the boats bumping the landing-stage becomes more and more frequent, he gets tied up in the chairs and has hardly enough time to go from one door to the other, for the bell is being rung almost continuously*]: Yes, straightaway ... did you put your pullover on? Yes, yes ... coming at once, be patient, yes, yes ... patience ...

OLD WOMAN: Your pullover? My pullover? ... sorry, sorry.

OLD MAN: This way, Ladies, Gentlemen, this way, *please* ... please ... sorry ... plea ... come in ... come in ... I'll take you ... there, the seats ... my dear friend ... not that way ... be careful ... you, a friend of mine! ...

   [*Then, for some time, not a word: just the continuous sound of waves, boats, and the bells being rung. The movement on the stage has reached a climax. All the doors now open and close ceaselessly. Only the large door at the back remains shut. The* OLD COUPLE *rush about from door to door, without saying a word; they look as though they are on roller-skates. The* OLD MAN *welcomes the guests, not accompanying them very far, just taking a few steps with them to show them where to sit; he has no time for more. The* OLD WOMAN *brings on chairs. Occasionally the* OLD COUPLE *meet and collide, without interrupting the general movement. Then, back-centre of the stage, the* OLD MAN *starts turning from left to right, right to left, etc., standing on the same spot and facing each door in turn; in the same way he points out seats to the guests, so quickly that his arm is whirling round at great speed. Similarly the* OLD WOMAN *stops, chair in hand, sets it down, picks it up, and sets it down again; from left to right, from right to left, it looks as if she too wishes to go to each door in turn, but only her face and neck are moving, at great speed. None of this should hold up the movement of the scene, as the* OLD COUPLE *must give the impression, although standing in the same place, that they have not stopped rushing about: the quick little gestures, circular perhaps, that they make with their hands, torso, head, and eyes should at last, very gradually begin to get slower; the bell-ringing not so loud, less frequent; the doors open less quickly. When finally the doors stop opening and shutting and there is no more bell-ringing, one should have the impression that the stage is overflowing with people.*]

OLD MAN: I'll find a place for you ... don't worry ... Semiramis, where the dickens ...

OLD WOMAN [*with a dramatic gesture; she is empty-handed*]: There aren't any more chairs, my love. [*Then she suddenly starts selling invisible programmes in the crammed auditorium, whose doors are all closed now.*] Programme! Programme! Would you like a programme, Sir? Programme, Madam?

OLD MAN: Don't you get excited, Ladies and Gentlemen, you'll all be attended to ... each one in turn, by order of arrival ... there'll be room for you all. We'll manage somehow.

OLD WOMAN: Programme! Programme! Just a moment, Madam, please! I can't serve everybody at once, I haven't got thirteen pairs of hands, I'm not a cow, you know ... Sir, I wonder if you'd mind passing this programme to the lady next to you? Thank you ... Change? No, I haven't any ...

OLD MAN: But I've told you we'll find you a seat! Don't get in such a state! This way, it's this way, there, be careful now ... Oh! How nice to see you ...

OLD WOMAN: Programme! Would you like ... Programme ... gramme ...

OLD MAN: Yes, my boy, she's down there, a little further down, selling programmes ... no such thing as a stupid job ... that's her ... seen her? ... there's a seat for you in the second row ... on the right ... no, on the left ... that's right!

OLD WOMAN: ... gramme ... gramme ... programme ... like programme ...

OLD MAN: Well, what else can I do? I'm doing my best! [*To some invisible seated guests*] Pull your chairs a little closer together, please ... a little more room there and you can sit down, Madam ... that's right. [*He is forced up on the platform by the pressure of the crowd.*] Ladies, Gentlemen, I am very sorry to announce that now it's standing room only ...

OLD WOMAN [*who is standing exactly opposite him, on the other side of the stage, between Door No. 3 and the window*]: Programme, programme! ... Would anyone like a programme? Choc ices, toffees ... acid drops ... [*Unable to move an inch, she is so pressed in by the crowd she has to throw her programmes and her sweets out at random over the heads of the invisible guests.*] Here you are! there you are!

OLD MAN [*standing on the platform, very excited; he is jostled down from the platform, struggles up again, is forced down, hits someone in the face and gets an elbow dug in his ribs; he says*]: So sorry ... Oh, I *am* sorry ... do be careful ... [*Knocked off his balance, he has a job to keep his feet and clings on to someone's shoulders.*]

OLD WOMAN: Who on earth are all these people? Programme, would you like a programme, choc ices?

OLD MAN: Ladies and Gentlemen, *please*! Silence for a

moment, I beg you! ... Quiet, please! ... an important announcement ... all those who have not been able to find seats are kindly asked to leave the gangways clear ... that's right ... don't stand between the chairs.

OLD WOMAN [*almost shouting to the Old Man*]: Who are all these people, my pet? What are they all doing here?

OLD MAN: Move to one side, Ladies and Gentlemen. Those who have no seats must not stand in front of the others, but should line up along the walls there, on the right and the left ... don't worry, you'll be able to see and hear everything, wherever you are!

[*There is a general shift round; pushed by the crowd the* OLD MAN *will move almost round the stage to end up by the window on the right, near the stool; the* OLD WOMAN *will do the same, but in the opposite direction, to end up by the stool near the window on the left.*]

OLD MAN [*as he carries out this movement*]: Don't push so, don't push.

OLD WOMAN [*as above*]: Don't push so, don't push.

OLD MAN [*as above*]: Don't push, don't!

OLD WOMAN [*as above*]: Ladies, don't push. Don't push, Gentlemen.

OLD MAN [*as above*]: Don't get excited ... there's no hurry ... gently, please ... what the ...

OLD WOMAN [*as before*]: Anyone would think you were a lot of savages.

[*At last they have arrived at their final positions, each one near a window; the* OLD MAN *on the left, by the window next to the platform, the* OLD WOMAN *on the right. They will not move again until the end.*]

OLD WOMAN [*calling to the Old Man*]: My pet ... I can't see you ... where are you? Who are they? What do all these people want? Who's that one?

OLD MAN: Where are you? Where are you, Semiramis?

OLD WOMAN: Where are you, my love?

OLD MAN: Here, next to the window ... can you hear me? ...

OLD WOMAN: Yes, I can hear your voice! And a lot of others, too, but I can pick yours out ...

OLD MAN: And you, where are you?

OLD WOMAN: I'm at the window, too! ... I feel frightened, my love, there are too many people here ... we're a long way from each other ... we ought to be careful, at our age ... we might get lost ... we must keep together, you never know, my love, my pet ...

OLD MAN: Hallo! ... I've just caught sight of you ... oh! ... we'll be together again, don't worry ... I'm with some friends. [*To the friends*] What a pleasure it is to shake hands with you again ... But of course, I believe in progress, steady progress, with set-backs obviously, and yet, and yet ...

OLD WOMAN: Quite well, thank you ... What terrible weather ... How beautiful it's been! [*Aside*] And yet I'm still frightened ... What am I doing here? ... [*Shouting*] My love, my pet! ...

[*Each of them talks to the guests separately.*]

OLD MAN: To prevent the exploitation of man by man, we need money, money, and still more money!

OLD WOMAN: My love! [*Then she is monopolized by friends.*] Yes, my husband's here, it's he who did the organizing ... over there ... Oh, you'll never reach him now ... you'd have to push your way through ... he's standing with friends ...

OLD MAN: Of course not ... that's what I've always said ... there's no such thing as pure logic ... it's all imitation.

OLD WOMAN: But you know there are some happy people. In the morning they breakfast in an aeroplane, they have their midday meal on a train and in the evening they dine at sea. They spend the night in lorries that go rumbling, rumbling, rumbling ...

OLD MAN: You talk about the dignity of man? At least, let's try to save his face. Dignity's only his back.

OLD WOMAN: Don't fall down in the dark. [*She bursts out laughing during the conversation.*]

OLD MAN: That's what your compatriots ask me.

OLD WOMAN: Certainly ... tell me all about it.

OLD MAN: I've called you all together ... to have it explained to you ... The person and the individual are one and the same person.

OLD WOMAN: There's something pinched about him. He's just out of prison for debt.

OLD MAN: I am not myself, I am someone else. I am the one in the other.

OLD WOMAN: Children, learn not to trust one another.

OLD MAN: Sometimes I wake up to find absolute silence around me. That's what I mean by the sphere. It's complete in itself. However, one has to be careful. The whole shape may suddenly disappear. There are holes it escapes through.

OLD WOMAN: Just ghosts, after all, nobodies, of no importance whatever ... My husband's duties are of supreme importance, quite sublime.

OLD MAN: I'm sorry to say I can't agree with you! ... I'll let you know what I think about all this in time ... I have nothing more to say just now! ... It's the Orator ... we're waiting for him at the moment – who'll answer for me, who'll explain to you exactly how we feel about everything ... he'll make it all clear ... when? ... when the right time comes ... you won't have to wait long now ...

OLD WOMAN [*to her friends*]: The sooner the better ... But of course ... [*Aside*] There's no peace for us now. If only they'd all go away! Where is my little pet? I can't see him any more ...

OLD MAN [*to his friends*]: Don't be so impatient. You'll hear what my message is. In a few minutes.

OLD WOMAN [*aside*]: Ah! ... I can hear his voice! ... [*To her friends*] Do you realize no one's ever understood my husband? His great moment has come at last.

OLD MAN: Listen! Experience of all kinds has deepened my knowledge of life and philosophy ... I am not a selfish man: I want all mankind to reap the benefit.

OLD WOMAN: Ouch! You're treading on my toes ... I've got chilblains!

OLD MAN: I have perfected my system in every detail. [*Aside*] The Orator ought to have come by now! [*Aloud*] I have suffered greatly.

OLD WOMAN: We have both suffered a great deal. [*Aside*] The Orator ought to have come by now. It's time he arrived.

OLD MAN: Suffered greatly and learnt a great deal.

OLD WOMAN [*like an echo*]: Suffered greatly and learnt a great deal.

OLD MAN: My system is perfect, you'll see for yourself.

OLD WOMAN [*like an echo*]: His system is perfect. You'll see for yourself.

OLD MAN: If only you are willing to follow my instructions.

OLD WOMAN [*echo*]: If only you'll follow his instructions.

OLD MAN: We must save the world! ...

OLD WOMAN [*echo*]: Save his own soul by saving the world! ...

OLD MAN: One truth for all men!

OLD WOMAN [*echo*]: One truth for all men!

OLD MAN: Do as I say!

OLD WOMAN [*echo*]: Do as he says!

OLD MAN: Because there's not a single doubt in my mind! ...

OLD WOMAN [*echo*]: Not a single doubt in his mind!

OLD MAN: *Never* ...

OLD WOMAN [*echo*]: Never, as long as you live ...

[*A great noise and a fanfare of trumpets are heard from the wings.*]

OLD WOMAN: What's happening?

[*The noise increases; then the door at the back opens wide, with a crash. Through the open door there is nothing to be seen, but a strong light floods the stage, coming through the big door and the windows, which are also brilliantly lit, as the Emperor arrives.*]

OLD MAN: I don't know ... it can't be ... it's not possible ... but yes ... it's incredible ... and yet ... yes ... why yes ... yes ... it's the Emperor! His Majesty the Emperor!

[*The light reaches its maximum intensity, flooding through the open door and the windows; but it is a cold, empty light; there is more noise, which stops abruptly.*]

OLD WOMAN: My love, my love ... who is it?

OLD MAN: Stand up! ... It's His Majesty the Emperor! The Emperor, in my house, in our house ... Semiramis ... do you realize?

OLD WOMAN [*not understanding*]: The Emperor ... the Emperor, my love? [*Then, suddenly she realizes.*] Ah yes! The Emperor! Your Majesty! Your Majesty! [*She starts curtseying wildly, grotesquely, a fantastic number of times.*] In our house! In our house!

OLD MAN [*weeping with emotion*]: Your Majesty! ... Oh! My Emperor! My great, my little Emperor! ... Oh! What a tremendous ... like a glorious dream ...

OLD WOMAN [*like an echo*]: Glorious dream ... glorious ...

OLD MAN [*to the invisible crowd*]: Ladies and Gentlemen! Rise to your feet! Our well-beloved Sovereign, our Emperor is among us! Hooray! Hooray! [*He gets up on the stool and stands on tip-toe to catch a glimpse of the Emperor: the* OLD WOMAN *does the same on her side of the stage.*]

OLD WOMAN: Hoorah! Hooray! [*Stamping of feet.*]

OLD MAN: Your Majesty! ... I'm here! ... Your Majesty!

Can you hear me? Can you see me? Well, tell His Majesty I'm here! Majesty! Majesty!!! I'm here, your most faithful servant! ...

OLD WOMAN [*still as echo*]: Your most faithful servant, Majesty!

OLD MAN: Your servant, your slave, your faithful hound, aouh! aouh! your hound, Majesty...

OLD WOMAN [*baying loudly, like a hound*]: Aouh ... aouh ... aouh ...

OLD MAN [*wringing his hands*]: Can you see me? Oh, answer me, Sire! ... Ah, I can see you, I've just caught a glimpse of your Majesty's imperial countenance ... that brow divine ... I have seen it, yes, in spite of the courtiers who screen you from view ...

OLD WOMAN: In spite of the courtiers ... we are here, Majesty.

OLD MAN: Majesty! Majesty! Ladies and Gentlemen, you can't let His Majesty remain standing ... you see, my Majesty, I'm really the only one who looks after you, who worries about your health. I am the most loyal of all your subjects ...

OLD WOMAN [*echo*]: We're your most loyal subjects!

OLD MAN: Well, let me get through, Ladies and Gentlemen ... how can I push my way through such a mob? ... But I must go and pay my humble respects to His Majesty the Emperor. ... Let me come through ...

OLD WOMAN [*echo*]: Let him go through ... let him pass ... through ... pass ...

OLD MAN: Let me through, let me get past then. [*Desperately*] Oh! Shall I ever reach him?

OLD WOMAN [*echo*]: Reach him ... reach him ...

OLD MAN: But I still lay my heart and my whole being at his feet; there's such a crowd of courtiers round him, oh dear, oh dear, they want to keep me from him ... they've a shrewd suspicion, all of them, that I'd ... Oh! I know them!

... I know all about Court intrigue ... they want to keep me
from Your Majesty.

OLD WOMAN: Don't upset yourself, my love ... His Majesty
can see you, he's looking at you ... His Majesty just winked
at me ... His Majesty is on our side! ...

OLD MAN: The best seat for His Majesty! ... near the platform
... so he can hear all the Orator says.

OLD WOMAN [*hoisting herself up on her stool and standing on
tip-toe, craning her neck up as high as she can, to have a better
view*]: Someone's looking after the Emperor at last.

OLD MAN: Thank Heaven for that! [*To the Emperor*] Sire ...
Your Majesty can trust that man, he's a friend of mine,
he's acting for me. [*Standing on the stool, on tip-toe*] Ladies
and Gentlemen, Children, little children, I implore you ...

OLD WOMAN [*echo*]: Plore ... plore ...

OLD MAN: ... I want to see ... move aside ... I want ... that
heavenly gaze, that imposing face, the crown, His Majesty's
radiance ... Sire, be pleased to turn your illustrious countenance towards your humble servant ... so very humble ...
oh! This time I can see quite clearly ... I can see ...

OLD WOMAN [*echo*]: He can see this time ... he can ... he can
see-ee-ee ...

OLD MAN: This is the height of happiness ... I have no words
to express the exceeding measure of my gratitude ... in my
simple dwelling, oh! Majesty! oh! Blazing sun! ... here ...
here ... in these quarters where I am, it's true, a General ...
though in the ranks of your army, I am just an ordinary
Quartermaster ...

OLD WOMAN [*echo*]: Quartermaster ...

OLD MAN: I feel proud, proud and humble at the same time ...
that's just as it should be ... alas! I'm a General, I know, but I
could have been at the Imperial Court, here my court is a
small backyard ... Majesty ... I ... Majesty, I don't express
myself very well ... I could have had ... a number of things,

possessed quite a lot of good things in life, if I'd only known, if I'd wanted to, if I ... if we ... Majesty, forgive my emotion ...

OLD WOMAN: The third person, you must use the third person!

OLD MAN [*maudlin*]: May Your Majesty condescend to forgive me! But you've come all the same ... we'd given up hoping ... we mightn't have been at home ... oh! saviour, in my life I have suffered humiliation ...

OLD WOMAN [*echo, sobbing*]: ... milia ... milia ...

OLD MAN: My life has been full of suffering. ... I could really have *been* someone, if only I could have counted on Your Majesty's support ... I have no one behind me ... it would all have been too late, if you hadn't come ... you are, Sire, my last hope in life ...

OLD WOMAN [*echo*]: Last hopeinlife ... Sire ... opeinlife ... p'inlife ...

OLD MAN: I have brought ill-luck to my friends, to all those who have helped me ... The lightning struck the outstretched hand ...

OLD WOMAN: ... stretched hand ... retched hand ... etched hand ...

OLD MAN: I have always been hated for the right reasons, and loved for the wrong ones ...

OLD WOMAN: That's not true, my pet, not true. You've got me to love you, to be your little mother ...

OLD MAN: All my enemies have been rewarded and my tried friends have betrayed me ...

OLD WOMAN [*echo*]: Tried ... trayed ... trayed ...

OLD MAN: They've wronged me and persecuted me. And if I complained, it was always *they* were proved right ... Sometimes I tried to revenge myself ... I could never, never do it. ... I had too much pity to lay the enemy low ... I've always been too good.

OLD WOMAN [*echo*]: He was too good, good, good, good, good ...

OLD MAN: Pity was my undoing.

OLD WOMAN [*echo*]: Pity ... pity ... pity ...

OLD MAN: But *they* had no pity. I would prick them with a pin; they'd attack me with their bludgeons, their knives, and their cannon, and mangle my bones ...

OLD WOMAN [*echo*]: ... bones ... bones ... bones.

OLD MAN: I was robbed of my positions, my possessions, my life ... I was a collector of disasters, a lightning conductor for catastrophe ...

OLD WOMAN [*echo*]: Conductor ... catastrophe ... astrophe ...

OLD MAN: In order to forget, Majesty, I tried to take up sport ... mountaineering ... my feet were pulled from under me ... when I tried to climb the stairs, I found the wood was rotten ... and the staircase collapsed ... when I wanted to travel, I was refused a passport ... when I wanted to cross the river, the bridges were blown ...

OLD WOMAN [*echo*]: Bridges were blown.

OLD MAN: I tried to cross the Pyrenees, but the Pyrenees weren't there.

OLD WOMAN [*echo*]: Pyrenees not there ... he too, Majesty, like so many others, could have been a General Editor, a Director-General, a General Physician, Majesty, or a Generalissimo ...

OLD MAN: And then, no one ever took any notice of me ... nobody ever sent me invitations ... and yet it was I, I tell you, it was I and I alone who could have saved mankind, suffering, sick mankind. Your Majesty understands this, as I do ... or at least I could have spared men the ills they have endured in the last twenty-five years, if only I had had the chance to pass on my message; I haven't given up hope of saving mankind, there is still time, and my plan is ready ... but I find it so difficult to express myself ...

OLD WOMAN [*shouting above the invisible heads*]: The Orator will be here, he'll speak for you ... His Majesty is here ... they'll hear your message, you needn't worry any more, you're holding all the trumps, it's not the same now, it's all different ...

OLD MAN: May Your Majesty forgive me ... with so many cares of State ... I have been humiliated ... Ladies and Gentlemen, move aside just a little, don't stand right under his Majesty's nose, I want to see the diamonds blazing in the Imperial Crown ... But if Your Majesty has been pleased to enter my poor dwelling, it must be because he deigns to show some regard for my unworthy self. What a wonderful recompense. Majesty, if physically speaking I am stretching up on the tips of my toes, it is not out of pride, but simply to behold your face! ... morally speaking, I am down on my knees before you ...

OLD WOMAN [*sobbing*]: At your knees, Sire, we are at your knees, at your feet, at your toes ...

OLD MAN: I once had scabies, Sire. My employer gave me the sack, because I would not bow down to his baby and his horse. I have been kicked in the backside, but none of that's important now, Sire ... because ... because ... Majesty ... look at me ... I am here ... here ...

OLD WOMAN [*echo*]: Here ... here ... here ... here ... here ... here ...

OLD MAN: Because Your Majesty is here ... because Your Majesty will heed my message ... But the Orator should be here ... He is keeping His Majesty waiting ...

OLD WOMAN: I beg Your Majesty to forgive him. He should be coming now. He'll be here in a moment. We've just had a telephone call.

OLD MAN: His Majesty is most kind. So His Majesty will not leave without having heard a word, he will stay to hear everything.

OLD WOMAN [echo]: Heard a word ... hear everything ...

OLD MAN: It is he who will speak in my name ... I'm afraid I can't ... I haven't the gift ... *he* has all the papers, all the documents ...

OLD WOMAN [echo]: He has all the documents ...

OLD MAN: A little patience, Sire, I beg you ... **he is just coming.**

OLD WOMAN: He'll be here in a moment.

OLD MAN [*so that the Emperor shall not grow impatient*]: Let me tell you, Majesty, how the revelation came to me a very long time ago ... I was forty years old ... I'm saying this for you, too, Ladies and Gentlemen ... one day, after the evening meal, I was sitting on my father's lap, as usual, before I went to bed ... my moustache was bigger than his, and more pointed ... my chest more hairy ... my hair already turning grey, his was still brown ... We had some visitors, grown-up people, at table and they started laughing, laughing.

OLD WOMAN [echo]: Laughing ... laughing ...

OLD MAN: This isn't a joke, I told them. I'm fond of my daddy. And they replied: It's midnight, and a youngster doesn't stay up so late. If you've not gone to bed yet, it's because you're a man, don't forget. I wouldn't have believed a word they said, if they hadn't talked about going to bed ...

OLD WOMAN [echo]: Bed.

OLD MAN: Instead of going bye-byes ...

OLD WOMAN: Bye-byes ...

OLD MAN: And then I thought: But I'm not married yet. So I must still be a child. And they married me off on the spot, just to prove I was wrong ... Luckily my wife has been a mother and a father to me ...

OLD WOMAN: The Orator should be here now, Majesty ...

OLD MAN: Just coming, the Orator.

OLD WOMAN: Just coming.

OLD MAN: Just coming.

OLD WOMAN: Just coming.

OLD MAN: Just coming.

OLD WOMAN: Just coming.

OLD MAN: Just coming, just coming.

OLD WOMAN: Just coming, just coming.

OLD MAN: Coming.

OLD WOMAN: Coming.

OLD MAN: Coming.

OLD WOMAN: Coming, he's here.

OLD MAN: Coming, he's here.

OLD WOMAN: Coming, he's here.

BOTH: He's here ...

OLD MAN: Here he is! ...

[*Silence. Not a movement. Turned to stone, the* OLD COUPLE *have their eyes fixed on Door No. 5; the stage remains quite still for a considerable time, about half a minute; then the door opens wide, silently and very, very slowly. The* ORATOR *appears: a real person. He looks like the typical painter or poet of the last century; a wide-brimmed black felt hat, a loosely tied cravat, an artist's jacket, moustache and goatee beard, rather a smug, pretentious look about him. If the invisible characters should appear as real as possible, the* ORATOR *should look unreal; slipping along the right-hand wall, he goes quietly to the back of the stage, in front of the great door, without moving his head to right or left; he passes close to the* OLD WOMAN *without seeming to notice her, even when she touches his arm to make sure he is really there; it is at this point that the* OLD WOMAN *says*]: Here he is!

OLD MAN: Here he is!

OLD WOMAN [*who has been following him with her eyes, and goes on doing so*]: He's here all right, he really exists. In flesh and blood.

OLD MAN [*watching him, too*]: He exists. And he's here all right. It's not a dream!

OLD WOMAN: It's not a dream. I told you it wasn't.

[*The* OLD MAN *clasps his hands and raises his eyes to Heaven; he is exulting, silently. When the* ORATOR *has reached the back of the stage, he removes his hat and bows in silence; he greets the invisible Emperor with a flourish of his hat, like one of the Musketeers and a little like a robot. Then*]

OLD MAN: Majesty ... may I present the Orator ...

OLD WOMAN: That's him!

[*Then the* ORATOR *puts his hat on again and mounts the platform. From there he looks down, over the heads of his invisible public, at the chairs; he freezes into a solemn pose.*]

OLD MAN [*to the invisible public*]: You may ask for his autograph.

[*Silently, automatically, the* ORATOR *signs and gives out countless autographs. Meanwhile the* OLD MAN *clasps his hands and raises his eyes again to Heaven in exultation*]

No man on earth can ask for more of life ...

OLD WOMAN [*echo*]: No man can ask for more.

OLD MAN [*to the invisible crowd*]: And now, with Your Majesty's permission, I should like to speak to you all, Ladies and Gentlemen, young children, my dear colleagues and fellow-countrymen all, Mr Chairman, comrades in arms ...

OLD WOMAN [*echo*]: Children in arms ... arms ... arms ...

OLD MAN: Speak to you all, without distinction of age, sex, civil status or social rank, of trade or profession, in order to thank you, from the bottom of my heart ...

OLD WOMAN [*echo*]: Thank you ...

OLD MAN: As I would thank the Orator, most warmly, for coming here in such great numbers ... Silence, Gentlemen! ...

OLD WOMAN [*echo*]: Silence, Gentlemen ...

OLD MAN: I should also like to thank all those who have made this meeting possible tonight, the organizers ...

OLD WOMAN: Hear! Hear!

[*Meanwhile, on the platform, the* ORATOR *is solemn and motionless, except for his hand, which goes on automatically signing autographs.*]

OLD MAN: The owners of this building, the architect, and the masons who were kind enough to raise these walls! ...

OLD WOMAN [*echo*]: ... walls ...

OLD MAN: All those who dug the foundations ... Silence, Ladies and Gentlemen ...

OLD WOMAN [*echo*]: ... dies and Gentlemen ...

OLD MAN: I wish to give particular thanks – for I am not forgetting them – to the joiners who made the chairs you're sitting on, to the skilful craftsman ...

OLD WOMAN [*echo*]: ... ilful ... aftsman ...

OLD MAN: ... who fashioned the armchair, in which Your Majesty so softly nestles, his mind still sharp and keen ... Thanks again to all the technicians, mechanics, electro-cutioners ...

OLD WOMAN [*echo*]: ... cutioners ... cutioners ...

OLD MAN: ... paper manufacturers and printers, proof-readers and editors, to whom we owe the programmes, so attractively adorned, I give thanks to the universal solidarity of the human race, thanks to our country, thanks to the State [*He turns in the direction of the Emperor.*] whose boat Your Majesty guides with the skill and knowledge of a true helmsman ... thanks to the programme-seller ...

OLD WOMAN [*echo*]: ... hapigram-seller ...

OLD MAN [*pointing to the Old Woman*]: ... for her sweets and ices ...

OLD WOMAN [*echo*]: ... sand-ices ...

OLD MAN: ... my wife and comrade ... Semiramis! ...

OLD WOMAN [*echo*]: ... ife ... com ... miss ... [*Aside*] Bless his heart, he never forgets to mention me.

OLD MAN: I should like to thank all those who, by their financial or moral encouragement, valuable and efficient support, have thus contributed to the phenomenal success of our celebration this evening ... thanks once more, and above all, to our well-loved Sovereign, His Majesty the Emperor ...

OLD WOMAN [*echo*]: ... jesty th' Emperor ...

OLD MAN [*in complete silence*]: ... Quiet, please ... Majesty ...

OLD WOMAN [*echo*]: ... ajesty ... jesty ...

OLD MAN: Majesty, my wife and myself have nothing more to ask of life. Our existence has found its final consummation ... Thanks be to Heaven that we have been granted so many long and peaceful years ... My life has been a full one. My mission is accomplished. I shall not have lived in vain, since my message is to be revealed to the world ... [*With a gesture to the* ORATOR, *who does not notice it; he is busy rejecting requests for autographs with a firm and dignified wave of the arm.*] To the world, or rather to what is left of it! [*Broad gesture to take in the invisible crowd*] To *you*, Ladies and Gentlemen, my dear friends, the left-over scraps of humanity, from which good soup can still be made ... My friend the Orator ... [*The* ORATOR *is looking somewhere else.*] If I have been misrepresented and misunderstood by my contemporaries for a long time now, it must have been ordained so ... [*The* OLD WOMAN *sobs.*] But what does all that matter now I can leave to you, dear friend and Orator [*The* ORATOR *repulses a fresh demand for an autograph; then strikes an attitude expressing indifference and gazes round on all sides.*] ... the task of dazzling posterity with the enlightenment I bring ... So make my philosophy known to the Universe. And do not omit the details of my private life, whether they're comical, painful or touching, my habits and my tastes, my gorgeous greed ... tell all you know ... speak of my dear companion [*The* OLD WOMAN *sobs still louder.*] ... of the way she used to prepare those marvellous little Turkish pasties of hers, and her rabbit *rillettes à la norman-dillette* ... and don't forget to mention Berry, where I was born ... I am looking to you, Master Orator ... as for me and my faithful spouse, after long years of labour in the cause of human progress, years in which we have fought for what is right and just, it only remains for us to withdraw from the scene ... and at once, in order to make the supreme sacrifice: no one demands it of us, nevertheless we are resolved ...

OLD WOMAN [*sobbing*]: Yes, yes, let us die in our moment of glory ... so that our names become legendary ... at least we shall have a street called after us ...

OLD MAN [*to the Old Woman*]: Oh! My faithful wife and companion! ... you who have believed in me, without a moment's doubt, for a whole century, who have never left my side, never ... today, alas, in our moment of triumph we are separated by a pitiless mob ...

> And yet I would
> Have found it good
> That you and I
> As one might lie
> Each bone to bone
> Beneath one stone
> Our old flesh breeding
> The same worms feeding
> Mouldering together ...

OLD WOMAN: ... mouldering together.

OLD MAN: Alas! ... Alack! ...

OLD WOMAN: Alas! ... Alack! ...

OLD MAN: ... Our bodies will fall far from one another, we shall rot in watery solitude ... Let us not complain too much.

OLD WOMAN: We must do what must be done! ...

OLD MAN: We shall not be forgotten. The eternal Emperor will always remember us, always.

OLD WOMAN [*echo*]: Always.

OLD MAN: We shall leave some trace behind, for we are not towns, but people.

BOTH [*together*]: A street will bear our names!

OLD MAN: Let us be united in time and eternity, if not in space, as we were in trial and tribulation; let us die at the same moment ... [*To the impassive, motionless Orator*] Once more, then ... I am depending on you ... You must tell everything.... Bequeath the message to everyone ... [*To the Emperor*] With Your Majesty's permission ... Farewell, to all of you. Farewell, Semiramis.

OLD WOMAN: Farewell, to all of you! ... Farewell, my love!

OLD MAN: Long live the Emperor! [*He throws confetti and paper streamers over the invisible Emperor; a fanfare of trumpets is heard; a brilliant light, as from a firework.*]

OLD WOMAN: Long live the Emperor! [*Confetti and paper streamers over the Emperor, then over the impassive, motionless Orator, and over the empty chairs*]

OLD MAN [*more confetti, etc.*]: Long live the Emperor!

OLD WOMAN [*more confetti, etc.*]: Long live the Emperor!

[THE OLD COUPLE *at one and the same time both jump through their windows, crying 'Long live the Emperor!' A sudden silence; the firework's glare has gone, an 'Ah!' is heard from both sides of the stage, and the glaucous sound of bodies striking water. The light is no longer coming through the great door and the windows: there is only the dim light there was at the beginning; the wide-open windows gape black, the curtains flapping in the wind.*

THE ORATOR, *who has remained motionless and impassive during the scene of the double suicide, decides after a few* moments' *effort to speak; as he faces the rows of empty chairs, he indicates to the invisible crowd that he is deaf and dumb; he uses sign-language; desperate efforts to make himself understood; then from his throat come moans and groans and the sort of guttural sounds made by deaf mutes.*]

He, Mme, mm, mm.

Ju, gou, hou, hou.

Heu, heu, gu, gou, gueu.

[*Helpless, his arms drop to his sides; suddenly his face lights up, he has an idea: he turns to the blackboard, takes a piece of chalk from his pocket, and writes in large capitals:*

ANGELBREAD*

then:

NNAA NNM NWNWNW V

He turns again to his invisible public, the public on the stage, and points to what he has written on the blackboard.]

ORATOR: Mmm, Mmm, Gueu, Gou, Gu, Mmm, Mmm, Mmm, Mmm.

[*Then, dissatisfied, he rubs out the chalk-marks with a series of sharp movements, and puts others in their place: among them the following can be discerned, in large capitals:*

ΛADIEU ΛDIEU ΛPΛ

Again the ORATOR *turns to the audience and smiles questioningly, as though he hopes he has been understood, has really said something; he points out to the empty chairs what he has just written; he waits, quite still, for a moment, looking fairly pleased and a little solemn; then, gradually, when the hoped-for reaction is not forthcoming, his smile disappears and his face clouds over; he waits a moment longer; then, suddenly, he bows moodily, abruptly, and comes down from the platform; he makes for the great door at the back with his ghostly walk; before he goes out through this door, he bows once more,*

* Translator's Note: ANGEPAIN in the original.

*ceremoniously, to the empty chairs and the invisible Emperor.
The stage is empty, apart from the chairs, the platform, and
the confetti and paper streamers over the floor. The door at
the back is wide open, gaping black.*

*For the first time human noises seem to be coming from the
invisible crowd; snatches of laughter, whisperings, a ' Ssh!' or
two, little sarcastic coughs; these noises grow louder and louder,
only to start fading away again. All this should last just long
enough for the real and visible public to go away with this
ending firmly fixed in their minds. The curtain falls very
slowly.]**

CURTAIN

* When first produced, the curtain fell during the moaning of the dumb
Orator. The blackboard was omitted.

THE LESSON

A Comic Drama

THE LESSON

First produced in Paris by Marcel Cuvelier at the Théâtre du Poche, 20 February 1951.

First produced in London by Peter Hall at the Arts Theatre Club, 9 March 1955.

Characters of the Play

THE PROFESSOR, *somewhere between fifty and sixty years of age*
THE GIRL PUPIL, *eighteen years old*
THE MAID, *between forty-five and fifty*

SCENE: *The old Professor's study, which is also his dining-room. On the left of the stage a door leads to the main staircase of the apartment block; at the back of the stage, on the right, another door opens on to a corridor in the flat.*

To the rear and slightly to the left there is a window hung with plain curtains, and outside, on the sill, pots of common or garden flowers.

In the distance can be glimpsed low red-roofed houses: the small town. The sky is bluish grey. On the right a simple dresser. The table, which also serves as a desk, stands in the centre of the room. Three chairs round the table, two more on either side of the window, a light wallpaper, a few shelves holding books.

> [*The stage is empty when the curtain goes up, but will not long remain so. The doorbell rings and the voice of the* MAID *is heard off-stage.*]

VOICE: Yes, yes. I heard you.

> [*The* MAID *is heard running down some steps off and then appears. A well-built woman, between forty-five and fifty, red-faced and wearing a peasant's cap. She comes in like a gust of wind, slamming behind her the door on the right, wiping her hands on her apron and running towards the door on the left, as a second ring is heard.*]

MAID: All right, all right, I'm coming.

> [*She opens the door. The* GIRL PUPIL, *aged eighteen, comes in. A grey apron, small white collar, a briefcase under her arm.*]

MAID: Good morning, Mademoiselle.

PUPIL: Good morning. Is the Professor at home?

MAID: Have you come for your lesson?

PUPIL: Yes, that's right.

MAID: He's expecting you. Sit down for a moment and I'll go and tell him.

PUPIL: Thank you.

[*She sits down at the table, facing the audience, her back turned to the door on the right, through which the* MAID *hurries out, calling*]

MAID: Will you come down, Sir, please? Your pupil has arrived.

[*The* PROFESSOR'S *rather piping voice is heard:*]

VOICE: Thank you, I'm coming ... in two minutes ...

[*The* MAID *has gone out. The* PUPIL, *like a good girl, settles down to wait, drawing her legs back under her chair, her briefcase on her knees: a glance or two round the room, at the furniture, at the ceiling too; then she takes a notebook out of her briefcase and turns the pages, stopping a little longer over one of the pages as though preparing a lesson, having a last run through her notes. She looks a polite, well brought-up girl, but vivacious, dynamic, and of a cheerful disposition: she has a bright smile. As the drama runs its course her general bearing and all her movements will gradually lose their animation, she will have to close up: she will slowly change from being happy and cheerful to being downcast and morose; after a lively start she will become more and more tired and sleepy: towards the end of the drama a state of nervous depression should be clearly apparent from her expression; it will make itself known by her way of speaking, her tongue becoming thick, words coming painfully back into her mind and just as painfully off her tongue: she will look as though she were vaguely paralysed, as though aphasia were setting in: self-willed at the beginning, almost to the point of being aggressive, she will become more and more passive, until she is nothing more than an object, limp and inert, lifeless, one would say, in the hands of the Professor: so that when the latter comes to make the final gesture, the*]

Pupil no longer reacts: rendered insensible, her reflexes no longer function: imprisoned in a motionless face, only her eyes can express her indescribable shock and terror: this transition from one state to another must of course be achieved by slow degrees, imperceptibly.

Enter the PROFESSOR. *A little old man with a pointed white beard: he wears pince-nez and a black skull-cap, a long black schoolmaster's gown, black trousers and black shoes, a white stiff collar and a black tie. Excessively polite, very shy, a voice subdued by his timidity, very correct, very professorial. He is constantly rubbing his hands together; now and again a prurient gleam, quickly dismissed, lights up his eyes. In the course of the drama his timidity will slowly and imperceptibly disappear; the prurient gleam in his eyes will end by blazing into an insistent, lecherous, devouring flame: apparently only too inoffensive at the beginning, the Professor will grow more and more sure of himself, excitable, aggressive, domineering, until he can do exactly as he pleases with his Pupil, she having become as putty in his hands. Obviously the Professor's voice too should change from thin and piping at the start, getting louder and fuller, to an extremely powerful, braying, sonorous instrument at the end; whereas the Pupil's voice, after being very clear and resonant at the beginning, will fade almost into inaudibility. During the opening passages the Professor could perhaps stutter slightly.*]

PROFESSOR: Good morning, good morning. ... You are ... er ... I suppose you really are ... er ... the new pupil?

[*The* PUPIL *turns round briskly and easily, very much the young lady: she gets up and goes towards the Professor, holding out her hand.*]

PUPIL: Yes, Sir. Good morning, Sir. You see I came at the right time. I didn't want to be late.

PROFESSOR: Good. Yes, that's very good. Thank you. But you shouldn't have hurried too much, you know. I don't know quite how to apologize to you for having kept you waiting. ... I was just finishing ... you understand, I was just ... er ... I do beg your pardon ... I hope you will forgive me. ...

PUPIL: Oh, but you mustn't, Sir. It's perfectly all right, Sir.

PROFESSOR: My apologies. ... Did you have any trouble finding the house?

PUPIL: Not a bit ... not a little bit. But then I asked the way. Everyone here knows you.

PROFESSOR: Yes, I've lived in the town for thirty years. I believe you have not been here very long. How do you like it?

PUPIL: Oh! I don't dislike it at all. It's a very pretty town, charming really, a nice park, a girls' boarding school – and then there's a bishop and lovely shops and streets and avenues. ...

PROFESSOR: Quite right ... Of course you're quite right. And yet, you know, I'd just as soon live somewhere else. Paris, for example, or at least Bordeaux.

PUPIL: Do you like Bordeaux, Sir?

PROFESSOR: I can't really say. I don't really know.

PUPIL: But do you know Paris?

PROFESSOR: Like ... er ... Bordeaux, you know, not exactly. But if you will allow me, could you perhaps tell me ... Paris, now, is the chief town of ... er ...?

[The PUPIL searches for a moment, then, pleased to know the answer]

PUPIL: Paris is the chief town of ... France?

PROFESSOR: But yes, of course, yes! Bravo! That's fine! That's excellent! I congratulate you. You have the geography of your country at your finger-tips. Your chief towns.

PUPIL: Oh, I don't know them all yet, Sir. It's not so easy as that, it's quite difficult to learn them.

PROFESSOR: It will come in time ... take heart, Mademoiselle ... I beg your pardon ... a little patience ... quietly, quietly does it ... you'll see, it will come. ... Beautiful weather we're having ... or perhaps not so ... er ... but after all why not? At least it's not too bad and that's the main thing ... er ... er ... it's not raining ... in fact it's not snowing, either.

PUPIL: That would be rather surprising in the summer.

PROFESSOR: Forgive me, Mademoiselle, I was just going to say that ... but you will learn that one has to be prepared for anything.

PUPIL: Yes, Sir. Naturally.

PROFESSOR: In this world of ours, Mademoiselle, one can never be sure of anything.

PUPIL: Snow falls in the winter. Winter is one of the four seasons. The other three are ... er ... sp ...

PROFESSOR: Yes, yes?

PUPIL: Spring ... and then summer ... and ... er ...

PROFESSOR: It begins like automobile, Mademoiselle.

PUPIL: Ah, yes! Autumn. ...

PROFESSOR: That's quite right, Mademoiselle. A very good answer. Excellent indeed. I am positive you will prove a very good pupil. You will make good progress. You are intelligent, you seem well-informed, good memory.

PUPIL: I really do know my seasons, don't I, Sir?

PROFESSOR: You do indeed, Mademoiselle ... or should I say almost. But it will come in time. And anyway, it's really not at all bad now. You'll come to know them all one day, all your seasons, with your eyes shut. Like me.

PUPIL: It's very difficult.

PROFESSOR: Not really. Only a little effort. A little good will, Mademoiselle. You'll see. It will come, I promise you.

PUPIL: Oh, I do hope so, Sir. I'm thirsty for knowledge. And then my parents too, they want most awfully for me to persevere in my studies. They would like me to specialize.

They believe that nowadays a little general culture, however soundly taught, just doesn't go far enough.

PROFESSOR: Mademoiselle, your parents are perfectly right. You must continue your studies. I apologize for saying so, but it is really quite essential. Modern life has become very complex.

PUPIL: And so complicated! ... Of course, I'm lucky, my parents aren't badly off. They'll be able to help me in my work, so that I can take the highest degrees there are.

PROFESSOR: And you would like to apply for an interview. ...

PUPIL: As soon as possible. To start working for my Doctor's Degree. It's in three weeks.

PROFESSOR: Let's see, now, if you'll allow me to put the question ... you already have your school-leaving certificate?

PUPIL: Yes, Sir. For Arts and Science.

PROFESSOR: Oh, but you're very well-developed – for your age. And what Doctorate do you wish to read for? Material science or normal philosophy?

PUPIL: My parents would really prefer me to read for all the Doctorates – if you think it's possible in such short a time.

PROFESSOR: All the Doctorates? ... You are a very courageous young lady. I really must congratulate you most sincerely. Well, we'll try, Mademoiselle, we'll do our best for you. Besides, you are most knowledgeable already. And so young, too.

PUPIL: Oh, Sir!

PROFESSOR: All right, then! We've hardly any time to lose. If you'll forgive me, if you'll be so kind ... perhaps we should make a start.

PUPIL: Not at all, Sir. Please don't apologize. I'm anxious to start.

PROFESSOR: Perhaps I could ask you then to be so kind as to take that chair ... that one there ... and if I may be permitted,

Mademoiselle, if you have no objection, I will take this one opposite you?

PUPIL: Certainly, Sir. But of course, please do.

PROFESSOR: Thank you, Mademoiselle.

[*They sit down opposite each other at the table, turning their profile to the spectators.*]

PROFESSOR: There we are then! You've brought your text-books and note-books with you?

[*The* PUPIL *takes them from her briefcase.*]

PUPIL: Yes, Sir. Of course, Sir. I've got all we need.

PROFESSOR: Excellent. That's excellent, Mademoiselle. Then, if you really don't mind ... we could ... begin?

PUPIL: Yes, Sir. I'm quite ready for you, Sir.

PROFESSOR: Ready for me? ... [*A gleam in the eye, quickly dispelled, a gesture immediately checked.*] It is I who am ready for you, Mademoiselle. I am at your service.

PUPIL: Oh, really, Sir ...

PROFESSOR: Well, then, if you ... er ... we ... er ... we, that is to say, I ... I'll begin by giving you a brief examination on the knowledge you have acquired so far, and that will give me an idea about the lines we must work on in the future. ... Good. How do you feel about your perception of plurality?

PUPIL: A little vague ... and confused.

PROFESSOR: Fine. We'll have a look at it.

[*He rubs his hands. The* MAID *comes in, and this seems to upset the* PROFESSOR. *She makes for the dresser, looks for something inside, and lingers.*]

Well now, Mademoiselle, what do you say to doing a little arithmetic ... that is, if you don't mind ...

PUPIL: But of course, Sir. Willingly. I couldn't ask for anything better.

PROFESSOR: It's a fairly new science, a modern science: strictly speaking I suppose one should call it a method rather than a science. ... It is also a therapy. [*To the Maid*] Marie, have you finished?

MAID: Yes, Sir. I've found the plate I was looking for. I'm just going. ...

PROFESSOR: Hurry up, please, and go back to the kitchen.

MAID: Yes, Sir, I'm going. [*Offers to go, then*] I beg pardon, Sir, but please be careful. Not too much excitement.

PROFESSOR: Don't be so ridiculous, Marie. Nothing whatever to worry about.

MAID: But that's what you always say.

PROFESSOR: Your insinuations are entirely without foundation. I am perfectly capable of behaving myself. After all, I'm old enough.

MAID: That's just it, Sir. You'd much better not start Mademoiselle off with arithmetic. That arithmetic never did anyone any good. It makes you tired and upsets you.

PROFESSOR: I'm too old for that now. And what business is it of yours, anyway? It's my concern and I know what I'm doing. You've no right to be here, anyway.

MAID: Very well, Sir. But don't you go telling me I didn't warn you.

PROFESSOR: I'm not interested in your warnings, Marie.

MAID: Monsieur must do as he thinks best.

[*She goes out.*]

PROFESSOR: I'm sorry about this stupid interruption, Mademoiselle. ... You must understand that this poor woman is always afraid I shall tire myself. She's worried about my health.

PUPIL: Oh, it really doesn't matter, Sir. It shows she's devoted to you. She must be very fond of you. Good servants are hard to find.

PROFESSOR: She really goes too far. It's stupid to be so nervous. Let us get back to our arithmetical sheep.

PUPIL: I follow you, Sir.

PROFESSOR [*wittily*]: But still sitting down, I see!

PUPIL [*appreciating the joke*]: Just like you, Sir!

PROFESSOR: Good! Then shall we arithmetize a little?

PUPIL: I'll be pleased to, Sir.

PROFESSOR: Then perhaps you wouldn't mind telling me ...

PUPIL: Not in the slightest, Sir. Please go ahead.

PROFESSOR: What do one and one make?

PUPIL: One and one make two.

PROFESSOR [*astounded by his pupil's erudition*]: But that's very good indeed! You're extremely advanced in your studies. You'll have very little difficulty in passing all your Doctorate examinations.

PUPIL: I'm very pleased to hear it, Sir. Especially from you.

PROFESSOR: Let us proceed a little further. What do two and one make?

PUPIL: Three.

PROFESSOR: Three and one?

PUPIL: Four.

PROFESSOR: Four and one?

PUPIL: Five.

PROFESSOR: Five and one?

PUPIL: Six.

PROFESSOR: Six and one?

PUPIL: Seven.

PROFESSOR: Seven and one?

PUPIL: Eight.

PROFESSOR: Seven and one?

PUPIL: Still eight.

PROFESSOR: Very good answer. Seven and one?

PUPIL: Eight again.

PROFESSOR: Excellent. Perfect. Seven and one?

PUPIL: Eight for the fourth time. And sometimes nine.

PROFESSOR: Magnificent! You're magnificent! Sublime! My

warmest congratulations, Mademoiselle. There's no point in going on. You're quite first-rate at addition. Let's try subtraction. Just tell me, that is if you're not too tired, what is left when you take three from four?

PUPIL: Three from four?... Three from four?

PROFESSOR: Yes, that's it. I mean to say, what is four minus three?

PUPIL: That makes ... Seven?

PROFESSOR: I'm extremely sorry to have to contradict you, but three from four doesn't make seven. You're muddling it up. Three plus four makes seven, take three away from four and that makes?... It's not a question of adding up, now you have to subtract.

PUPIL [*struggling to understand*]: Yes ... I see. ...

PROFESSOR: Three from four, that makes ... How many ... how many?

PUPIL: Four?

PROFESSOR: No, Mademoiselle. That's not the answer.

PUPIL: Three then?

PROFESSOR: That's not right either, Mademoiselle. ... I really do beg your pardon ... It doesn't make three ... I'm terribly sorry ...

PUPIL: Four minus three ... three away from four ... four minus three? I suppose it wouldn't make ten?

PROFESSOR: Oh, dear me, no, Mademoiselle. But you mustn't rely on guesswork, you must reason it out. Shall we try and solve it together? Would you be so good as to count?

PUPIL: Yes, Sir. One ... two ... three ...

PROFESSOR: You know how to count all right? You can count up to what number?

PUPIL: I can count up to ... infinity.

PROFESSOR: That's impossible.

PUPIL: Up to sixteen, then.

PROFESSOR: That's quite far enough. We must all recognize our limitations. Go on counting then, if you please.

PUPIL: One ... two ... and then after two comes three ... four ...

PROFESSOR: Stop there, Mademoiselle. Which number is the greater? Three or four?

PUPIL: Er ... three or four? Which is the greater? The greater number out of three and four? In what way greater?

PROFESSOR: Some numbers are smaller than others. In the greater numbers there are more units than there are in the smaller ones.

PUPIL: Than in the smaller numbers? ...

PROFESSOR: Unless, of course, the small numbers are made up of smaller units. If all the units are very small, there may be more units in the small numbers than in the big ones ... that is, if they are not the same units. ...

PUPIL: In that case small numbers can be bigger than big numbers?

PROFESSOR: Yes, well, we won't go into that. That would take us much too far: I just want you to realize that there are other things apart from numbers ... there are sizes, too, and totals, and then there are groups and heaps, heaps of things, like ducks and drakes and cabbages and kings, etc. ... etc. ... Let us just suppose, to make it easier, that the numbers we're dealing with are all of the same kind, then the greatest numbers will be those that have the most units, assuming all the units are of the same kind too.

PUPIL: The one that has the most will be the greatest? Now I understand, Sir, you are equating quality with quantity.

PROFESSOR: That's a little too theoretical, Mademoiselle, too theoretical. You don't need to worry about that. Let us take an example and think it out in that particular case. Our general conclusions can come later. We have the number four and the number three, each one having a number of identical units. Which number will be the greater, the smaller number or the greater number?

PUPIL: I'm sorry, Sir ... but what do you mean by the greater number? Is it the one that is less small than the other one?

PROFESSOR: That's it, Mademoiselle. Exactly. You've understood perfectly.

PUPIL: Then it must be four.

PROFESSOR: What is four? Greater or smaller than three?

PUPIL: Smaller ... no, greater.

PROFESSOR: Excellent answer. How many units are missing between three and four? ... or between four and three, if you'd rather?

PUPIL: There aren't any units, Sir, between three and four. Four comes immediately after three; there is nothing at all between three and four!

PROFESSOR: I can't have made myself understood properly. It's doubtless my own fault. I haven't been clear enough.

PUPIL: Oh, no, Sir. The fault is entirely mine.

PROFESSOR: Listen. Here are three matches. And here is another one. That makes four. Now, watch carefully. There are four of them. I take one away, how many do you have left?

[*Neither the matches, nor any of the objects in question are visible: the* PROFESSOR *will get up from the table, write on an imaginary blackboard with imaginary chalk, etc.*]

PUPIL: Five. If three and one make four, four and one make five.

PROFESSOR: No, that's not right, not right at all. You have a constant predilection for adding up. But it is also necessary to subtract. Integration alone is not enough. Disintegration is essential too. That's what life is. And philosophy. That's science, progress, civilization.

PUPIL: Yes, Sir.

PROFESSOR: Let us get back to our matches. I have four of

them then. You can see that there are four all right. I take
one away, and that leaves me with ...

PUPIL: I don't know, Sir.

PROFESSOR: Come now. Think a little. It's not easy, I admit.
And yet you're clever enough to make the intellectual effort
required and succeed in understanding. Well, then?

PUPIL: I don't seem to, Sir. I really don't know, Sir.

PROFESSOR: All right, we'll take some simpler examples. If
you had two noses and I'd plucked one off, how many
would you have left?

PUPIL: None.

PROFESSOR: What do you mean, none?

PUPIL: Well, it's just because you haven't plucked one off
that I've still got one now. If you had plucked it off, it
wouldn't be there any more.

PROFESSOR: You didn't quite understand my example.
Suppose you had only one ear.

PUPIL: Yes, and then?

PROFESSOR: I stick on another one, how many would you
have?

PUPIL: Two.

PROFESSOR: Good. I stick yet another one on. How many
would you have?

PUPIL: Three ears.

PROFESSOR: I take one of them away ... how many ears ...
do you have left?

PUPIL: Two.

PROFESSOR: Good. I take another one away. How many do
you have left?

PUPIL: Two.

PROFESSOR: No. You have two ears. I take away one. I
nibble one off. How many do you have left?

PUPIL: Two.

PROFESSOR: I nibble one of them off. One of them. ...

PUPIL: Two.

PROFESSOR: One.

PUPIL: Two.

PROFESSOR: One!

PUPIL: Two!

PROFESSOR: One! !

PUPIL: Two! !

PROFESSOR: One! !

PUPIL: Two! !

PROFESSOR: One! !

PUPIL: Two! !

PROFESSOR: No, no, no. That's not it at all. The example is not ... is not convincing enough. Listen to me.

PUPIL: Yes, Sir.

PROFESSOR: You have ... er ... you have ... er ...

PUPIL: Ten fingers! ...

PROFESSOR: Good! If you like. Fine! You have ten fingers, then.

PUPIL: Yes, Sir.

PROFESSOR: How many would you have if you had five of them?

PUPIL: Ten, Sir.

PROFESSOR: No, that's wrong!

PUPIL: But I should, Sir.

PROFESSOR: I tell you you're wrong!

PUPIL: But you've just told me that I have ten ...

PROFESSOR: And then I told you immediately afterwards that you had five!

PUPIL: But I haven't got five, I've got ten!

PROFESSOR: Let us proceed in a different way. ... Let us, for the purpose of subtraction, limit ourselves to the numbers one to five. ... A little patience, Mademoiselle, and you'll see. I'm going to help you to understand. [*The* PROFESSOR *begins to write on an imaginary blackboard. He draws it up nearer the* PUPIL, *who turns round to see it.*] Now watch, Mademoiselle ... [*He pretends to be drawing on the blackboard: one stick. Then he appears to write underneath the figure 1; then two sticks, and under them the figure 2. Then still lower down the figure 3, and finally he draws four sticks, under which he writes the figure 4.*]

You can see all right? ...

PUPIL: Yes, Sir.

PROFESSOR: These are all sticks, Mademoiselle, sticks, you understand? This is one stick; then there are two sticks; one, two, three sticks in all; then four sticks, five sticks, and so on. One stick, two sticks, three sticks, four and five sticks, those are numbers. When you count the sticks, each stick is a unit, Mademoiselle ... Repeat what I've just said!

PUPIL: 'A unit, Mademoiselle! Repeat what I've just said!'

PROFESSOR: Either figures, or numbers! One, two, three, four, five, the elements of numeration, Mademoiselle.

PUPIL [*hesitantly*]: Yes, Sir. Elements, figures that are sticks; units and numbers ...

PROFESSOR: At one and the same time ... that is to say, in point of fact, the whole of arithmetic boils down to that.

PUPIL: Yes, Sir. Very good, Sir. Thank you, Sir.

PROFESSOR: Now then, you can count, if you like, making use of these elements ... add up and subtract ...

PUPIL [*trying to fix it in her memory*]: The sticks are figures and numbers, units.

PROFESSOR: Hm ... in a manner of speaking. And then what?

PUPIL: You can subtract two units from three units, but can you subtract two twos from three threes? And two figures from four numbers? And three numbers from one unit?

PROFESSOR: No, Mademoiselle. You cannot.

PUPIL: But why not, Sir?

PROFESSOR: Just because, Mademoiselle.

PUPIL: Because what, Sir? Since they're all the same?

PROFESSOR: That's just the way things are, Mademoiselle, it can't be explained. You understand it by a sort of mathematical sense inside you. Either you've got it or you haven't.

PUPIL: There's nothing can help me, then!

PROFESSOR: Listen, Mademoiselle! If you don't succeed in fully understanding these archetypal arithmetical principles, you'll never succeed in carrying out your work properly as a polytechnician. And what's more, no one will be able to put you in for a course at a polytechnic school ... or even an establishment for infants. I confess it is by no means easy, it's obvious that it's very very abstract ... but if you've not mastered these elementary propositions, how can you ever hope to make mental calculations such as – and this would be as easy as winking to an average engineer – such as this, for example: how much is three billion, seven hundred and fifty-five million, nine hundred and ninety-eight thousand, two hundred and fifty-one, multiplied by five billion, one hundred and sixty-two million, three hundred and three thousand, five hundred and eight?

PUPIL [*very rapidly*]: That makes nineteen quintillion, three hundred and ninety quadrillion, two trillion, eight hundred and forty-four billion, two hundred and nineteen million, a hundred and sixty-four thousand, five hundred and eight. ...

PROFESSOR [*astonished*]: No, I don't think so. That must make nineteen quintillion, three hundred and ninety quadrillion, two trillion, eight hundred and forty-four billion, two hundred and nineteen million, a hundred and sixty-four thousand, five hundred and nine ...

PUPIL: No ... five hundred and eight ...

PROFESSOR [*growing more and more astonished and calculating in his head*]: Yes ... you're right, by Jove ... yours is the correct product ... [*Muttering unintelligibly*] ... quintillion, quadrillion, trillion, billion, million ... [*Distinctly*] ... a hundred and sixty-four thousand, five hundred and eight ... [*Stupefied*] But how did you arrive at that, if you don't understand the principles of arithmetical calculation?

PUPIL: Oh! It's quite easy, really! As I can't depend on reasoning it out, I learnt off by heart all the possible combinations in multiplication.

PROFESSOR: But the combinations are infinite!

PUPIL: I managed to do it, anyway!

PROFESSOR: It's quite astounding! ... Nevertheless, you will allow me to point out to you that I am by no means satisfied, Mademoiselle, and you must do without my congratulations; in mathematics, and particularly in arithmetic, what counts – and you can't get away from counting in arithmetic – what counts above all else is the ability to understand what you are doing. ... You ought to have found the answer by a dual process of inductive and deductive mathematical reasoning, and that is the way you should arrive at all your answers. Memory is a deadly enemy to mathematics, and though it has certain advantages, arithmetically speaking, memory is a bad thing! ... and so I'm not at all happy about you ... that just won't do at all ...

PUPIL [*crushed*]: No, Sir.

PROFESSOR: We'll forget about it for the moment. Let us pass on to another kind of exercise ...

PUPIL: Yes, Sir.

MAID [*as she comes in*]: Hm! ... Hm! ... Monsieur! ...

PROFESSOR [*not hearing her*]: It's a great pity, Mademoiselle, that you're not more advanced in special mathematical studies ...

MAID [*pulling at his sleeve*]: Monsieur! Monsieur!

PROFESSOR: I am afraid you can hardly think of going in for the total Doctorates ...

PUPIL: Oh, what a shame, Sir!

PROFESSOR: At least, if you ... [*To the Maid*] Leave me alone,

Marie, what on earth do you think you're up to? Back to
the kitchen and your washing up! Go on! Go on! [*To the
Pupil*] Still, we'll try to prepare you at least for the partial
Doctorate ...

MAID: Monsieur! ... Monsieur! ... [*Pulling at his sleeve.*]

PROFESSOR [*to the Maid*]: For goodness' sake, let me go!
Leave me alone! What the devil do you mean by it? ... [*To
the Pupil*] I think perhaps I should teach you then, if you're
really anxious to go in for the partial Doctorate ...

PUPIL: Oh yes, please, Sir!

PROFESSOR: ... the essentials of linguistics and comparative
philology ...

MAID: No, Monsieur, no! ... I shouldn't do that if I were
you! ...

PROFESSOR: Marie! Now you're really going too far!

MAID: Of all things, not philology, Monsieur, philology is
the worst of all ...

PUPIL [*surprised*]: The worst of all? [*Smiling a little stupidly*]
What a funny thing to say!

PROFESSOR [*to the Maid*]: That's too much! Leave the room!

MAID: Very well, Monsieur, very well. But you won't say I
didn't warn you! Philology is the worst of all!

PROFESSOR: I am over twenty-one, Marie!

PUPIL: Yes, Sir.

MAID: Monsieur must do as he thinks best! [*She goes out.*]

PROFESSOR: Shall we go on, Mademoiselle?

PUPIL: Please, Sir.

PROFESSOR: I shall ask you then to follow this prepared course
of mine with the closest attention ...

PUPIL: Yes, Sir!

PROFESSOR: ... thanks to which you may, in fifteen minutes,
acquire the fundamental principles of the comparative and
linguistic philology of the neo-Spanish languages.

PUPIL: Oh, Sir! How marvellous! [*Clapping her hands*]

PROFESSOR [*with authority*]: Silence! What's all this for?

PUPIL: I'm sorry, Sir! [*Slowly, she lays her hands on the table again.*]

PROFESSOR: Silence! [*He gets up and paces the room, his hands behind his back; now and again he stops, in the centre of the room or close to the Pupil, and reinforces his words with a gesture of the hand; he declaims his lecture, but without overdoing it; the* PUPIL *follows him with her eyes, sometimes with difficulty, for she is always having to twist her head round; once or twice, but no more, she makes a complete turn.*] Spanish, then, Mademoiselle, is actually the mother language that gave birth to all the neo-Spanish languages, among which we include Spanish, Latin, Italian, our own French, Portuguese, Rumanian, Sardinian or Sardanapalus, Spanish and neo-Spanish, and in certain respects we may add Turkish, itself however rather closer to Greek, which is after all perfectly logical, Turkey being Greece's neighbour and Greece lying closer to Turkey than either you or I: this is but one more illustration of a very important linguistic law, according to which geography and philology are twins ... You may take notes, Mademoiselle.

PUPIL [*in a strangled voice*]: Yes, Sir!

PROFESSOR: What distinguishes the neo-Spanish languages one from the other and separates them from other linguistic groups, such as the group comprising the Austrian and neo-Austrian or Hapsburgian languages, or such groups as the Esperantist, Helvetic, Monegasque, Swiss, Andorran, Basque, Pelota, not to speak of the diplomatic and technical language groups – what distinguishes them, I say, is their striking resemblance to one another, so that it is extremely difficult to tell them apart – I am speaking of the neo-Spanish languages themselves, which, however, can be differentiated, thanks to their distinctive characteristics, unquestionable and indisputable evidence of that remarkable resemblance that renders their common origin indisputable and, at the same time, clearly 'differentiates them – through the conservation of those distinctive characteristics I have just mentioned.

PUPIL: Oooh! Oooooh, Sir!

PROFESSOR: But let us not linger over generalities ...

PUPIL [*regretfully, fascinated*]: Oh, Sir ...

PROFESSOR: You seem to be interested in this. All the better.

PUPIL: Oh yes, Sir, I am ...

PROFESSOR: Don't worry, Mademoiselle. We shall come back to it later ... unless of course we don't come back to it at all. Who can say?

PUPIL [*delighted anyway*]: Oh yes, Sir.

PROFESSOR: Every language, Mademoiselle – note this carefully, and remember it *till the day you die* ...

PUPIL: Oh! yes, Sir, till the day I die ... Yes, Sir ...

PROFESSOR: ... and again, this is another fundamental principle, every language is in fact only a manner of speaking, which inevitably implies that it is made up of sounds, or ...

PUPIL: Phonemes ...

PROFESSOR: I was just about to say so. Don't show off, airing your knowledge! You'd better just listen.

PUPIL: Very well, Sir. Yes, Sir.

PROFESSOR: Sounds, Mademoiselle, should be caught in flight by their wings so that they do not fall on deaf ears. Consequently, when you have made up your mind to articulate, you are recommended, in so far as possible, to stretch your neck and your chin well up, and stand right on the tips of your toes, look now, like this, you see ...

PUPIL: Yes, Sir.

PROFESSOR: Be quiet. Sit where you are. Don't interrupt ... and to let the sounds out as loud as you can, with the full force of your lungs, assisted by your vocal cords. Like this.

Watch me: 'Butterfly', 'Eureka', 'Trafalgar', 'Pepper-pot'. In this way the sounds, filled with warm air weighing lighter than the air all around, will float on and on, no longer in danger of falling on deaf ears, bottomless pits that are the veritable graves of lost sonorities. If you emit several sounds at an increased speed, they will automatically grapple on to one another, thus constituting syllables, words, phrases if need be, and by that I mean groupings of more or less importance, sounds arranged in a purely irrational way, devoid of all sense, and yet for that very reason able to maintain themselves in the upper air, without risk of falling, at quite high altitudes. Only words that are charged with significance, heavy with meaning, dive downwards and always succumb in the end, crumpling up and ...

PUPIL: ... falling on deaf ears.

PROFESSOR: Quite right, but don't interrupt ... and in indescribable chaos ... or bursting like balloons; and so, Mademoiselle ...

[*The* PUPIL *suddenly looks as if she were in pain.*]

What's the matter with you?

PUPIL: I've got toothache, Sir.

PROFESSOR: No matter, we're not stopping for a little thing like that. To continue ...

PUPIL [*whose toothache goes on getting more and more painful*]: Yes, Sir. I've got toothache.

PROFESSOR: To continue.

PUPIL: Yes.

PROFESSOR: Summing up, then; learning to pronounce takes years and years. Thanks to science, we can do it in a few minutes. So that we can make sounds and words and anything you like; you must realize then that the air has to be pitilessly forced out of the lungs and then made to pass gently over the vocal cords, lightly brushing them, so that like harps or leaves beneath the wind, they suddenly start quivering, trembling, vibrating, vibrating, vibrating or hissing, or rustling, or bristling, or whistling, and with a whistle set everything in motion: uvula, tongue, palate, teeth ...

PUPIL: I've got toothache.

PROFESSOR: ... lips ... Finally words come out through the nose, the mouth, the ears, the pores of the skin, bringing in their train all the uprooted organs of speech we've just named, a powerful, majestic swarm, no less than what we improperly call the voice, modulating in song or rising in terrible symphonic wrath, a regular procession, sheaves of assorted blossoms, of sonorous conceits: labials, dentals, plosives, palatals, and the rest, some soft and gentle, some harsh and violent.

PUPIL: Yes, Sir. I've got toothache.

PROFESSOR: We go on. We go on. As for the neo-Spanish languages, they are such very near relations that we might almost think of them as second cousins. Moreover, they have the same mother: Spanish, the 'h' is unaspirated. That is why it is so difficult to tell one from the other. That is why it helps so much to pronounce properly, to avoid mistakes in pronunciation. Pronunciation is in itself worth a whole dialect. Bad pronunciation can play you some funny tricks. Allow me, while we're on this subject, to tell you a little personal story, in parenthesis. [*Slight relaxation. For a moment the* PROFESSOR *gives himself up to his memories; his expression becomes sentimental; but he quickly recovers himself.*] It was when I was very young, little more than a child perhaps. I was doing my military service. I had a friend in the regiment, a viscount, who had a rather serious speech defect: he was unable to pronounce the letter 'f'. Instead of saying 'f', he used to say 'f'. If he wanted to say: fresh fields and pastures new, he would say: fresh fields and pastures new. He pronounced filly as filly; he said Franklin instead of Franklin, fimblerigger instead of fimblerigger, fiddlesticks instead of fiddlesticks, funny face instead of funny face, Fe Fi Fo Fum instead of I smell the blood of an Englishman; Philip instead of Philip; fictory instead of fictory; February instead of February; April-May instead of April-May; Galeries Lafayette and not, as it should be pronounced, Galeries Lafayette; Napoleon instead of Napoleon, etcetera instead of etcetera and so on etc. ... Only he was lucky enough to be able to conceal the defect so well, thanks to his choice of hats, that no one ever noticed it.

PUPIL: Yes. I've got toothache.

PROFESSOR [*quickly changing his tone of voice*]: Let us go on. We shall first examine the points of similarity, so that later on we may the better understand what distinguishes these languages from one another. The differences are scarcely perceptible to anyone not experienced in detecting them. Thus all words in all languages ...

PUPIL: Oh yes? ... I've got toothache.

PROFESSOR: We go on ... are always the same, as are all flexional endings, all prefixes, all suffixes, all roots ...

PUPIL: Are the roots of words square roots?

PROFESSOR: Square or cubic. It depends.

PUPIL: I've got toothache.

PROFESSOR: To continue. And so, to give you an example, which is barely more than an illustration, take the word 'front'.

PUPIL: How am I to take it?

PROFESSOR: How you like, so long as you take it, but whatever you do, don't interrupt.

PUPIL: I've got toothache.

PROFESSOR: Let us continue ... I said: Let us continue ... Take the word 'front' then. Have you taken it?

PUPIL: Yes, yes. I've got it. Oh, my tooth, my tooth ...

PROFESSOR: The word 'front' is the root word in frontispiece. Also in effrontery. 'Ispiece' is a suffix, and 'ef' a prefix. They are so called because they do not alter. They don't want to.

PUPIL: I've got toothache.

PROFESSOR: To continue. Quickly now. These prefixes are of Spanish origin, I sincerely hope you realized that?

PUPIL: Oh! How my tooth aches!

PROFESSOR: To continue. You must also have noticed that they are the same in French and even in English. All right, Mademoiselle, there's no way of altering them in Latin, Italian, or Portuguese either; nor in Sardanaple or Sardana-politan, in Rumanian, neo-Spanish, Spanish, nor even in Oriental; front, frontispiece, effrontery; always and invariably the same word, with the same root, same suffix, same prefix in all the above-mentioned languages. And it's the same story for every word.

PUPIL: Those words mean the same thing in all languages? I've got toothache.

PROFESSOR: Exactly. Besides, it's really more a concept than a word. In any case you always have the same meaning, the same composition, the same structure of sound, not only in this word, but in all the words you can conceive, in every language. For each single concept is expressed by one and the same word and its synonyms, in all the countries of the world. Oh, leave your tooth alone!

PUPIL: I've got the toothache! I have, I have, I have, I have.

PROFESSOR: Good. Let us go on. I said: Let us go on ... How, for example, would you say, in English, the roses of my grandmother are as yellow as my grandfather who was born in Asia?

PUPIL: Toothache! Toothache! Toothache!

PROFESSOR: Come along now, that doesn't stop you saying it!

PUPIL: In English?

PROFESSOR: In English.

PUPIL: Er ... you want me to say in English: the roses of my grandmother are ...

PROFESSOR: ... as yellow as my grandfather who was born in Asia ...

PUPIL: Well then, one would say, in English, I think: the roses ... of my ... How do you say grandmother in English?

PROFESSOR: In English? Grandmother.

PUPIL: The roses of my grandmother ... yellow, in English, you say yellow?

PROFESSOR: Yes, of course!

PUPIL: Are as yellow as my grandfather when he lost his temper.

PROFESSOR: No! ... who was born ...

PUPIL: In Asia ... I've got toothache.

PROFESSOR: That's right.

PUPIL: I've got ...

PROFESSOR: Toothache ... never mind ... let's go on! Now I'd like you to translate the same sentence into Spanish, and then into neo-Spanish ...

PUPIL: In Spanish ... it must be: the roses of my grandmother are as yellow as my grandfather who was born in Asia.

PROFESSOR: No, that's quite wrong.

PUPIL: And in neo-Spanish: the roses of my grandmother are as yellow as my grandfather who was born in Asia.

PROFESSOR: Wrong! Wrong! Wrong! You've mixed them up. You've mistaken Spanish for neo-Spanish and neo-Spanish for Spanish ... Ah ... No ... it's just the other way round ...

PUPIL: I've got toothache and you're muddling everything up.

PROFESSOR: It's you who are muddling me up. You should

be more attentive. I'll say the sentence in Spanish, and then in neo-Spanish, and lastly in Latin. You must repeat them after me. Be very careful, for the similarity is surprising. The similarities are identical. Listen and follow me carefully ...

PUPIL: I've got ...

PROFESSOR: Toothache.

PUPIL: Let us go on ... Ah! ...

PROFESSOR: ... in Spanish: the roses of my grandmother are as yellow as my grandfather who was born in Asia; in Latin: the roses of my grandmother are as yellow as my grandfather who was born in Asia. Do you catch the distinction? Translate that sentence into Rumanian.

PUPIL: The ... how do you say roses in Rumanian?

PROFESSOR: Come, come! Roses, of course.

PUPIL: I thought it might be roses! Oh! How my tooth aches ...

PROFESSOR: No, no, how could it be? Since in Oriental roses is the translation of the French word roses and of the Spanish roses. Have you grasped it? In Sardanapol: roses ...

PUPIL: I'm terribly sorry, Sir, but ... Ooh! How my tooth aches! ... I don't hear any difference.

PROFESSOR: But it's so simple! So perfectly simple! It's merely a question of practice, of having a certain technical experience in the diverse languages, so very diverse in spite of the identical characteristics they share. I'll try and give you a key ...

PUPIL: Toothache!

PROFESSOR: What distinguishes these languages is neither the words, which are all absolutely the same, nor the structure of the sentences, which is similar in each case, nor the intonation, which offers no variation, nor the rhythm of speech ... what distinguishes them ... are you listening to me?

PUPIL: I've got the toothache.

PROFESSOR: Will you listen to me, Mademoiselle? Aah! You're making me very angry.

PUPIL: And I've had enough of it, Sir! I've got toothache.

PROFESSOR: Damn and blast you! Will you listen to me!

PUPIL: Oh, all right ... yes, I'll listen ... I'll try ... go on ...

PROFESSOR: What distinguishes them one from the other, on the one hand, Spanish, with the 'h' unaspirated, the mother language, on the other hand ... is ... is ...

PUPIL [*pulling a face*]: Is what?

PROFESSOR: Is an intangible thing. An intangible thing you can only grasp after a certain length of time, after much difficulty and long experience ...

PUPIL: Really?

PROFESSOR: Yes, really, Mademoiselle. There are no rules for it. You've got to have the knack, that's all there is to it. And to have the knack needs study, study, and still more study.

PUPIL: Toothache.

PROFESSOR: There are, however, certain particular cases in which the words do vary from one language to the next ... but we cannot use these examples as a basis for our studies, as they are, to all intents and purposes, exceptional.

PUPIL: Are they really, Sir? ... Oh, Sir, I've got toothache.

PROFESSOR: Don't interrupt! And don't make me angry! For if I lose control of myself ... As I was saying, then ... Ah, yes, those exceptional cases which are said to be easily distinguishable ... or easily differentiated ... or conveniently distinct, if you prefer ... I repeat: if you prefer, for I notice that you are no longer paying attention ...

PUPIL: I've got the toothache.

PROFESSOR: As I was saying, then: certain words, employed in certain expressions in current use, differ totally from one language to another, with the result that the language spoken is, in such cases, easier to identify. I will give you an example: the neo-Spanish expression, widely heard in Madrid: 'my country is neo-Spain', becomes in Italian: 'my country is ...'

PUPIL: Neo-Spain.

PROFESSOR: No! 'My country is Italy'. Just tell me now, by a simple process of deduction, how you say 'Italy' in French?

PUPIL: I've got the toothache!

PROFESSOR: Yet it's not at all difficult, for the word 'Italy' we have in French the word 'France', which is an exact translation. My country is France. And France in Oriental becomes the Orient! My country is the Orient. And the Portuguese for Orient is Portugal! Thus, the Oriental expression: my country is the Orient becomes, when translated into Portuguese: my country is Portugal! And so on and so on ...

PUPIL: That's enough! That's enough! I've got ...

PROFESSOR: The toothache! The toothache! ... Teeth, teeth, teeth! ... I'll have them all out for you in a minute ... Here is another example. The word 'capital' takes on a different meaning according to the language one is speaking. So that if a Spaniard says: 'I live in the capital', the word 'capital' won't have the same meaning at all as it has for a Portuguese who uses the same expression: 'I live in the capital.' And the same applies to a Frenchman, a neo-Spaniard, a Rumanian, a Latin, or a Sardanapolitan ... As soon as you hear someone say, Mademoiselle, Mademoiselle, I'm saying this for your benefit, blast you! As soon as you hear the expression: I live in the capital, you will know at once and without difficulty whether it is Spanish, or neo-Spanish, or French, or Oriental, or Rumanian, or Latin, for you merely have to guess what capital the person who makes the remark is thinking about, at the very moment he pro-

nounces the word ... But these are about the only precise
examples I can give you ...

PUPIL: Oh Lord! My tooth ...

PROFESSOR: Silence! Or I'll blow your brains out!

PUPIL: Just you try! Windbag!

[*The* PROFESSOR *takes her by the wrist and twists it.*]
Ouch!

PROFESSOR: Be quiet, then! I don't want to hear a word from
you!

PUPIL [*snivelling*]: Toothache ...

PROFESSOR: The most ... how should I say ... the most ...
paradoxical ... yes, that's the word ... the most paradoxical
thing is that hundreds of people who are completely lack-
ing in education speak these different languages ... Did you
hear? What have I just said?

PUPIL: ... speak these different languages! What have I just
said!

PROFESSOR: You were lucky that time! ... The lower classes
speak a Spanish, sprinkled, unbeknown to them, with neo-
Spanish words, while all the time they think they are
talking Latin ... or else they speak a Latin, sprinkled with
Oriental words, while under the impression they are talking
Rumanian ... or a Spanish sprinkled with neo-Spanish,
while firmly convinced it is Sardanapol or Spanish ... Are
you following me?

PUPIL: Yes! Yes! Yes! I am! What more do you want ...

PROFESSOR: Not so much cheek, my poppet, or you'd better
look out ... [*Very angrily*] But to cap it all, Mademoiselle,
those who say, for example, in a Latin they take to be
Spanish: 'I've got pains in my chilblains', are as perfectly
well understood by a Frenchman who doesn't know a word
of Spanish as though he were being addressed in his own
language. What is more, he believes it is his own language.
And the Frenchman will reply in French, like this: 'I too

have got pains in my chilblains', and he'll make himself understood perfectly well by the Spaniard, who will be positive the remark was made in the best Spanish and that Spanish is the language that is being spoken ... whereas, in reality, it is neither Spanish nor French, but Latin as spoken by a neo-Spaniard ... Why can't you keep still, Mademoiselle? Stop shifting your legs about and stop stamping your feet!

PUPIL: I've got the toothache.

PROFESSOR: How does it come about that while the lower classes talk without knowing what language they're speaking, while each person actually believes he is speaking a language that, in fact, he is not, they all somehow manage to communicate satisfactorily with one another?

PUPIL: Wonders will never cease.

PROFESSOR: It is simply one of the inexplicable and quaint peculiarities of the vulgar empiricism of the plebs – not to be confused with experience! – a paradox, a curious little sidelight, one of the little oddities of human nature, a part of its whimsical freakishness, and in point of fact, what comes into play here is quite simply, and in one word, nothing more or less, than instinct.

PUPIL: Ha! Ha!

PROFESSOR: It would be better if you could keep your eyes off the flies, while I'm giving myself all this trouble for you ... it would help if you tried to be a little more attentive ... I'm not the one who's taking the partial Doctorate ... I passed mine long ago ... my *total* Doctorate, in fact ... *and* my super-total diploma ... Can't you understand that I'm only trying to help you?

PUPIL: Toothache!

PROFESSOR: No manners! ... But it can't go on like this, not like this, not like this, not like this ...

PUPIL: I'm ... paying ... attention ...

PROFESSOR: At last! In order to learn to distinguish all these different languages, I've already said that there's nothing like practice ... Let us proceed in an orderly fashion. I'll try to teach you all the possible translations of the word 'Knife'.

PUPIL: All right, if you want to ... After all ...

PROFESSOR [calling the Maid]: Marie! ... Marie! ... She can't hear me ... Marie! ... Marie! ... Oh really! ... Marie! [He opens the door on the right.] Marie! ...

    [He goes out. The PUPIL is left alone for a few minutes, gazing blankly into space, quite besotted.]

[From outside in a shrill voice] Marie! What's the meaning of this? Why don't you come when I want you? You know you must come at once when I call! [He returns, followed by the MAID.] I'm the one who gives the orders here, you understand? [Pointing to the Pupil] This girl doesn't understand anything. Not a thing!

MAID: Don't take on so, Monsieur, think what it may lead to! It'll take you further than you want to go, you'll go too far, you know.

PROFESSOR: I shall be able to stop in time.

MAID: I've heard that before. I'd like to see it happen.

PUPIL: I've got the toothache.

MAID: What did I tell you! It's beginning! That's the sign!

PROFESSOR: What sign? What do you mean? What are you talking about?

PUPIL [in a flabby voice]: Yes, what are you talking about? I've got the toothache.

MAID: It's the final symptom! The worst symptom!

PROFESSOR: Nonsense! Nonsense! Nonsense!

    [The MAID makes to leave.]

Don't go away like that! I called you to go and look for the knives: the Spanish, neo-Spanish, Portuguese, French,

Oriental, Rumanian, Sardanapolitan, Latin, and Spanish ones.

MAID [*severely*]: You needn't think you can count on me.

[*She goes out. The* PROFESSOR *makes a movement of protest, then controls himself, rather at a loss. Suddenly he remembers.*]

PROFESSOR: Ah! [*He goes quickly to the drawer and finds a big imaginary knife; he takes hold of it and brandishes it exultantly.*] Here's one, Mademoiselle, here's a knife! It's a pity this is the only one; but we'll try to make it serve for all the languages! All you need to do is to pronounce the word Knife in each language, while you stare closely at the object and imagine it belongs to the language you're using.

PUPIL: I've got the toothache.

PROFESSOR [*almost chanting, melodiously*]: Come along then: Say Kni, like Kni, Fff, like Fff ... and watch it carefully, don't take your eyes off it ...

PUPIL: What is it, this one? French, Italian, or Spanish?

PROFESSOR: It doesn't matter ... It doesn't matter to you. Say: Kni.

PUPIL: Kni.

PROFESSOR: Fff ... Watch it. [*He moves the knife in the Pupil's face.*]

PUPIL: Fff ...

PROFESSOR: Again ... Watch it.

PUPIL: No! No! No more! That's enough! I've had enough! Besides, my teeth ache and my feet ache and my head aches ...

PROFESSOR: Knife ... Watch it ... Knife ... Watch it ... Knife ... Watch it ...

PUPIL: You make my ears ache, too. What a voice you've got! How piercing it is!

PROFESSOR: Say Knife ... Kni ... Fff ...

PUPIL: No, no! My ears are aching. I'm aching all over ...

PROFESSOR: I'll soon have those little ears of yours off, my poppet, and then they won't hurt you any more ...

PUPIL: Ow! You're hurting me, it's you that's hurting me ...

PROFESSOR: Look, come along now, quick, say it after me: Kni ...

PUPIL: Oh, if I must ... Kni ... Knife ... [*A moment of lucidity, of irony*] It must be neo-Spanish ...

PROFESSOR: If you like. Yes, it is neo-Spanish, but hurry up now ... we haven't got much time ... And what are you insinuating! You're getting too big for your shoes!

[*The* PUPIL *should be growing more and more tired and desperate, more and more tearful, at once distraught and exalted.*]

PUPIL: Ah!

PROFESSOR: Say it again, watch it. [*Like a child*] Knifey ... Knifey ... Knifey ... Knifey ...

PUPIL: Oh, my head! ... My head aches ... [*She passes her hand over each part of her body as she names it, like a caress.*] ... my eyes ...

PROFESSOR [*like a child*]: Knifey ... Knifey ... Knifey ... [*They are both standing: he, still brandishing his invisible knife, almost beside himself, and turning about her as though executing a sort of scalp dance; but nothing must be exaggerated and the Professor's steps are barely indicated: the* PUPIL, *standing face to the public, moves backwards towards the window, languorous, ailing, spellbound ...*]

Say it again, say it: Knife ... Knife ... Knife ...

PUPIL: I'm aching all over ... my throat, neck ... ah ... my shoulders ... my breasts ... knife ...

PROFESSOR: Knife ... Knife ... Knife ...

PUPIL: My hips ... Knife ... My thighs ... Kni ...

PROFESSOR: Say it clearly ... Knife ... Knife ...

PUPIL: Knife ... my throat ...

PROFESSOR: Knife ... Knife ...

PUPIL: Knife ... my shoulders ... my arms, my breasts, my hips ... knife ... knife ...

PROFESSOR: That's right ... now you're saying it nicely ...

PUPIL: Knife ... my breasts ...

PROFESSOR [*in a different voice*]: Take care ... don't break my window panes ... the knife can kill ...

PUPIL [*in a weak voice*]: Yes, yes ... the knife can kill?

[*The* PROFESSOR *kills the Pupil with a spectacular thrust of the knife.*]

PROFESSOR: Aaaah! There!

[*She too cries out, then falls, crumpling into an immodest position on the chair which happens to be in the right place near the window: they both cry out, murderer and victim, at the same moment. After the first knife-thrust the* PUPIL *has fallen on to the chair, her legs apart and hanging on either side of it: the* PROFESSOR *remains standing in front of her, back to the public; after the first blow, he gives the dead Pupil a second thrust of the knife, with an upward movement; and then he starts visibly and his whole body shudders.*]

PROFESSOR [*out of breath, stammering*]: Trollop ... She asked for it ... Now I feel better ... Ah! Ah! I'm tired ... I can hardly breathe ... Ah! [*He is breathing with difficulty: he falls. Luckily there is a chair to catch him; he wipes his forehead, mutters something unintelligible; his breathing becomes more normal ... He rises to his feet, looks at the knife in his hand, looks at the girl, then, as though he were waking up, panic-stricken*] What have I done! What will happen to me now? What will come of it all? Oh, dear, oh, dear! How awful! Mademoiselle! Get up, Mademoiselle! [*He turns about, still holding in his hand the invisible knife he does not know how to dispose of.*] Come along, Mademoiselle, the lesson is over now ... You can go home ... you can pay me another time ... Oh! She's *dead* ... dead ... And with my knife ...

She's *dead* ... It's terrible. [*He calls the Maid.*] Marie! Marie! Oh Marie, come quickly! Ah! Ah!

[*The door on the right half-opens.* MARIE *appears.*]

No! ... Don't come in ... I made a mistake ... I don't want you, Marie ... I don't need you any more ... you understand?

[MARIE *comes in, looking very severe. She looks at the body and says nothing.*]

[*His voice less assured*] I don't really need you, Marie ...

MAID [*sarcastically*]: So you're pleased with your pupil, then? She learnt a lot from her lesson?

PROFESSOR [*hiding his knife behind his back*]: Yes, the lesson is over now ... but ... she ... she's still here ... she won't go away ...

MAID [*not sympathetically*]: Well, well!

PROFESSOR [*quivering*]: It wasn't me ... I didn't do it ... Marie ... No ... I promise you ... it wasn't me, Marie ... dear Marie ...

MAID: Who was it, then? Who else was it? Me?

PROFESSOR: I don't know ... perhaps ...

MAID: Or was it the cat?

PROFESSOR: Perhaps it was ... I don't know ...

MAID: And it's the fortieth time today! And every day it's the same story! Every day! Aren't you ashamed of yourself, at your age too! ... but you'll go and make yourself ill! There soon won't be any more pupils left. And a good thing, too.

PROFESSOR [*vexed*]: It's not my fault! She wouldn't learn anything! She was disobedient! She was a bad pupil! She didn't want to learn!

MAID: Liar!

PROFESSOR [*approaching the Maid slyly, his knife behind his back*]: It's none of your business! [*He tries to strike her a terrific blow, but she seizes his wrist and twists it; the* PROFESSOR *drops his knife.*] ... Forgive me!

[*The* MAID *strikes the* PROFESSOR *twice, forcibly and noisily, so that he falls to the ground on his behind, snivelling.*]

MAID: You little murderer! Revolting little swine! Wanted to do that to me, did you! I'm not one of your blessed pupils! [*She hauls him up by the back of his collar, picks up his skull-cap, and puts it back on his head. He is afraid of being hit again and protects himself with his elbow, like a child.*] Put the knife back where you found it! Come along now!

[*The* PROFESSOR *puts it back in the drawer of the dresser and comes back to her.*]

And I gave you proper warning, too, only a little while ago! Arithmetic leads to Philology, and Philology leads to Crime ...

PROFESSOR: You said Philology was the worst of all!

MAID: It all comes to the same in the end.

PROFESSOR: I didn't quite understand. I thought when you said Philology was the worst of all, you just meant it was the hardest to learn ...

MAID: Liar! Old fox, you! A clever man like you doesn't go making mistakes about what words mean. You can't fool me!

PROFESSOR [*sobbing*]: I didn't kill her on purpose!

MAID: At least you're sorry you did it?

PROFESSOR: Oh yes, Marie, I swear I am.

MAID: I can't help feeling for you. Come now! You're not a bad boy after all! We'll try and do what we can to put things right. But don't you go doing it again ... Why, it could give you heart trouble ...

PROFESSOR: Yes, Marie! ... What are we going to do then?

MAID: We're going to bury her ... at the same time as the other thirty-nine ... forty coffins that'll make ... we're going to call in the undertakers and my boy-friend Auguste, the priest ... we're going to order the wreaths ...

PROFESSOR: Yes. Thank you, Marie, very much.

MAID: Come to think of it, it's hardly worth asking Auguste, not when you're a bit of a priest yourself, when you want to be, if you can believe what people say.

PROFESSOR: Not too dear, though, the wreaths. She hasn't paid for her lesson.

MAID: Don't worry ... better just cover her with her apron, anyway; she's not decent. And then we'll carry her away.

PROFESSOR: Yes, Marie, yes. [*He covers her.*] Could get sent to jail for this, you know ... forty coffins ... Just think of it ... People *would* be surprised ... What if anyone asks us what's inside?

MAID: Don't go making trouble for yourself. We'll say they're empty. Besides, no one will ask any questions. They're used to it.

PROFESSOR: All the same ...

MAID [*bringing out an armband bearing a device, the Swastika perhaps*]: Here you are! Put this on, if you're frightened, then you won't have anything to be afraid of. [*She puts it round his arm.*] ... It's political.

PROFESSOR: Thank you, thank you, kind Marie; I feel much safer like that ... You're a good girl, Marie ... You're a good girl, Marie ... very faithful ...

MAID: That's all right. Well, Monsieur? Are you ready?

PROFESSOR: Yes, Marie. I'm ready.

[*The* MAID *and the* PROFESSOR *take the young girl's body, one by the shoulders, the other by the legs, and go towards the door on the right.*]

Take care, now, not to hurt her.

[*They go out. The stage is empty a few moments. A ring at the bell at the door on the left.*]

VOICE OF THE MAID: I'm coming! Just a minute!

[*She appears as at the beginning of the play and goes towards the door. The bell rings a second time.*]

MAID [*to herself*]: She's in a good old hurry, this one! [*Aloud*]

Coming! [*She goes to the door and opens it.*] Good morning, Mademoiselle. Are you the new pupil? You've come for your lesson? The Professor's expecting you. I'll go and tell him you've arrived. He'll be down in a minute! Come in, won't you, Mademoiselle!

CURTAIN

READ MORE IN PENGUIN

In every corner of the world, on every subject under the sun, Penguin represents quality and variety – the very best in publishing today.

For complete information about books available from Penguin – including Puffins, Penguin Classics and Arkana – and how to order them, write to us at the appropriate address below. Please note that for copyright reasons the selection of books varies from country to country.

In the United Kingdom: Please write to *Dept. EP, Penguin Books Ltd, Bath Road, Harmondsworth, West Drayton, Middlesex UB7 ODA*

In the United States: Please write to *Consumer Sales, Penguin USA, P.O. Box 999, Dept. 17109, Bergenfield, New Jersey 07621-0120.* VISA and MasterCard holders call 1-800-253-6476 to order Penguin titles

In Canada: Please write to *Penguin Books Canada Ltd, 10 Alcorn Avenue, Suite 300, Toronto, Ontario M4V 3B2*

In Australia: Please write to *Penguin Books Australia Ltd, P.O. Box 257, Ringwood, Victoria 3134*

In New Zealand: Please write to *Penguin Books (NZ) Ltd, Private Bag 102902, North Shore Mail Centre, Auckland 10*

In India: Please write to *Penguin Books India Pvt Ltd, 706 Eros Apartments, 56 Nehru Place, New Delhi 110 019*

In the Netherlands: Please write to *Penguin Books Netherlands bv, Postbus 3507, NL-1001 AH Amsterdam*

In Germany: Please write to *Penguin Books Deutschland GmbH, Metzlerstrasse 26, 60594 Frankfurt am Main*

In Spain: Please write to *Penguin Books S. A., Bravo Murillo 19, 1° B, 28015 Madrid*

In Italy: Please write to *Penguin Italia s.r.l., Via Felice Casati 20, I–20124 Milano*

In France: Please write to *Penguin France S. A., 17 rue Lejeune, F–31000 Toulouse*

In Japan: Please write to *Penguin Books Japan, Ishikiribashi Building, 2–5–4, Suido, Bunkyo-ku, Tokyo 112*

In South Africa: Please write to *Longman Penguin Southern Africa (Pty) Ltd, Private Bag X08, Bertsham 2013*

PENGUIN AUDIOBOOKS

A Quality of Writing That Speaks for Itself

Penguin Books has always led the field in quality publishing. Now you can listen at leisure to your favourite books, read to you by familiar voices from radio, stage and screen. Penguin Audiobooks are produced to an excellent standard, and abridgements are always faithful to the original texts. From thrillers to classic literature, biography to humour, with a wealth of titles in between, Penguin Audiobooks offer you quality, entertainment and the chance to rediscover the pleasure of listening.

You can order Penguin Audiobooks through Penguin Direct by telephoning (0181) 899 4036. The lines are open 24 hours every day. Ask for Penguin Direct, quoting your credit card details.

A selection of Penguin Audiobooks, published or forthcoming:

Little Women by Louisa May Alcott, read by Kate Harper

Emma by Jane Austen, read by Fiona Shaw

Pride and Prejudice by Jane Austen, read by Geraldine McEwan

Beowulf translated by Michael Alexander, read by David Rintoul

Agnes Grey by Anne Brontë, read by Juliet Stevenson

Jane Eyre by Charlotte Brontë, read by Juliet Stevenson

The Professor by Charlotte Brontë, read by Juliet Stevenson

Wuthering Heights by Emily Brontë, read by Juliet Stevenson

The Woman in White by Wilkie Collins, read by Nigel Anthony and Susan Jameson

Nostromo by Joseph Conrad, read by Michael Pennington

Tales from the Thousand and One Nights, read by Souad Faress and Raad Rawi

Robinson Crusoe by Daniel Defoe, read by Tom Baker

David Copperfield by Charles Dickens, read by Nathaniel Parker

The Pickwick Papers by Charles Dickens, read by Dinsdale Landen

Bleak House by Charles Dickens, read by Beatie Edney and Ronald Pickup

Anna Karenina by Fyodor Dostoyevsky, read by Juliet Stevenson

PENGUIN AUDIOBOOKS

READ MORE IN PENGUIN

Penguin Twentieth-Century Classics offer a selection of the finest works of literature published this century. Spanning the globe from Argentina to America, from France to India, the masters of prose and poetry are represented by the Penguin.

If you would like a catalogue of the Twentieth-Century Classics library, please write to:

Penguin Marketing, 27 Wrights Lane, London W8 5TZ

(Available while stocks last)

READ MORE IN PENGUIN

A CHOICE OF TWENTIETH-CENTURY CLASSICS

Orlando Virginia Woolf

Sliding in and out of three centuries, and slipping between genders, Orlando is the sparkling incarnation of the personality of Vita Sackville-West as Virginia Woolf saw it.

Selected Poems Patrick Kavanagh

One of the major figures in the modern Irish poetic canon, Patrick Kavanagh (1904–67) was a post-colonial poet who released Anglo-Irish verse from its prolonged obsession with history, ethnicity and national politics. His poetry, written in an uninhibited vernacular style, focused on the 'common and banal' aspects of contemporary life.

More Die of Heartbreak Saul Bellow

'One turns the last pages of *More Die of Heartbreak* feeling that no image has been left unexplored by a mind not only at constant work but standing outside itself, mercilessly examining the workings, tracking the leading issues of our times and the composite man in an age of hybrids' – *New York Book Review*

Tell Me How Long the Train's Been Gone James Baldwin

Leo Proudhammer, a successful Broadway actor, is recovering from a near-fatal heart attack. Talent, luck and ambition have brought him a long way from the Harlem ghetto of his childhood. With Barbara, a white woman who has the courage to love the wrong man, and Christopher, a charismatic black revolutionary, Leo faces a turning-point in his life.

Memories of a Catholic Girlhood Mary McCarthy

Blending memories and family myths, Mary McCarthy takes us back to the twenties, when she was orphaned in a world of relations as colourful, potent and mysterious as the Catholic religion. 'Superb ... so heartbreaking that in comparison Jane Eyre seems to have got off lightly' – Anita Brookner

READ MORE IN PENGUIN

A CHOICE OF TWENTIETH-CENTURY CLASSICS

The Prodigy Hermann Hesse

Hesse's early novel *The Prodigy* is based on his own experiences of a narrow and uncaring education. Hans Giebenrath is a gifted child and the victim of provincial ambitions. Sent to theological school, the intelligent and imaginative boy is gradually driven to nervous collapse in a situation from which there seems to be no escape.

Something Childish and Other Stories Katherine Mansfield

'The singular beauty of her language consists, partly, in its hardly seeming to be language at all, so glass-transparent is it to her meaning. Words had but one appeal for her, that of speakingness' – Elizabeth Bowen

Collected Poems 1947–1985 Allen Ginsberg

Leading poet of the Beat generation, spokesman for the anti-war generation, an icon of the counter-culture, Allen Ginsberg remains an authentically American voice. This volume brings together four decades of bold experiment and provocative verse from *Howl*, one of the most widely read poems of the century, to his later, highly acclaimed collection, *White Shroud*.

Incest Anaïs Nin

Spanning the years 1932–4, the material in *Incest* was considered too explosive to include when the journals were originally published. In it, Nin reveals her incestuous affair with her pianist father, and recounts other relationships, loves and desires.

The Last Summer Boris Pasternak

Pasternak's autobiographical novella is a series of beautifully interwoven reminiscences, half-dreamed, half-recalled by Serezha, an intensely romantic young man and former tutor to a wealthy Moscow family. Here he broods over the last summer before the First World War, 'when life appeared to pay heed to individuals, and when it was easier and more natural to love than to hate'.